Private Keepers of the Public Interest

Private Keepers
of the Public Interest

Paul T. Heyne

ASSOCIATE PROFESSOR OF ECONOMICS
SOUTHERN METHODIST UNIVERSITY

McGraw-Hill Book Company

NEW YORK   ST. LOUIS   SAN FRANCISCO   TORONTO
LONDON   SYDNEY

Private Keepers of the Public Interest

To Julie, My Colleague

Preface

This book is an economic, political, and ethical critique of current conceptions of the businessman's social responsibilities. "It is a foolish thing," says the Second Book of Maccabees, "to make a long prologue, and to be short in the story itself." Since the story will be short, the prologue should be brief. But the dangers of misunderstanding are so great in this area, and actual misinterpretation so common, that it seems prudent to begin with some words of caution, disclaimer, and apology.

The essential concepts and the fundamental notions from which this book proceeds have been developed and explored by a number of writers on economics, ethics, and public policy. But they have seldom been brought together in brief compass, and hence the light which they shed on the perplexing issue of the businessman's social responsibilities has not been adequately focused. The problem is not so much that we lack the knowledge to extricate ourselves from an impasse as that we have failed to employ the knowledge which we already possess. This book is above all an attempt at critical integration.

But it is at the same time a contentious piece. The reader may even conclude part way through that the book is a sustained assault upon ethics, and a defense of immorality and irresponsibility in the business world. Nothing could be farther from the writer's intention. It *is* important that men be ethical; it may well be of very special importance to our society that its *businessmen* be ethical. "The behaviour of the community," Alfred North Whitehead once said, "is largely dominated by the business mind. A great society is a society in which its men of business think greatly of their functions. Low thoughts mean low behaviour, and after a brief orgy of exploitation low behaviour means a descending standard of life." [1] The writer wholeheartedly agrees with this judgment.

But as Whitehead suggests, thought comes before behavior. The businessman must *think greatly* of his functions. And that is one of the principal concerns of this book. What a man *is* will in the long run prove more important than what he *does*. Yet most of the discussion about ethics and social responsibility in the business community is narrowly confined to conduct, to particular decisions, to practical problems. It is bad enough that discussion in this vein has failed even to resolve the questions with which it has dealt; what is far worse is that such discussion has distracted attention from the more fundamental problem. Being precedes doing. This short sentence contains, in the writer's opinion, a truth of profound importance.

On the other hand, we must certainly concern ourselves directly and immediately with doing. The conduct of businessmen has consequences which we cannot ignore, consequences that are political as well as economic. But we have too often examined the issues of conduct and consequences

---

[1] Alfred North Whitehead, *Adventures of Ideas* (The Macmillan Company, New York, 1933), p. 124. Copyright 1933, 1961 by The Macmillan Company.

with a dangerous myopia. By fixing our gaze firmly in one spot we have been able to propose solutions that raise more problems than they resolve. Broader economic questions and fundamental political principles have been largely ignored in our zeal to make businessmen "socially responsible."

"About things on which the public thinks long it commonly attains to think right." Perhaps Samuel Johnson was overly optimistic when he wrote that. In any event, a contentious book is more likely than an unclear one to stimulate longer thinking.

An author's debts are always too numerous to mention. Some of them are indicated in the Bibliographical Note at the end of the book. Among those who have kindly given their permission to quote, we are especially grateful to the *Harvard Business Review,* a journal that has done much to improve the quality of discussion in this area. Raymond C. Baumhart's pioneering study of contemporary ethical attitudes among businessmen, first published in the journal's "Problems in Review," contributed more to this book than either Father Baumhart or the present author might care to admit.

I am also much indebted to my former students in the Graduate School of Business Administration at the University of Illinois. Their interest in the problems of business and society forced me to clarify my own thinking, and their friendly criticism had much to do with whatever persuasiveness the book possesses.

But the most friendly and helpful critic has been my wife. Her role as coauthor is inadequately but gratefully reflected in the dedication.

PAUL T. HEYNE

Contents

I.

In Quest of a Definition

W hat are the social responsibilities of the businessman? To judge by the number of books, articles, conferences, pronouncements, and even college courses dealing with this question, the businessman's social responsibilities are a matter of urgent concern today.

When viewed in historical perspective, this is a surprising development. The most determined critics of business are usually willing to admit that today's businessman typically pays more attention to his social responsibilities than did his forebears of a century or even a generation ago. Since a crime commission is rarely organized when the crime rate is low and falling, why are we currently witnessing an intensified interest in the question of socially responsible business behavior?

Several explanations for this paradox suggest themselves.

Perhaps we have come to expect more of the business-man. One corollary of the cold war is a certain anxious interest in the relative performance of the American and Soviet economies, and this, in the view of many, confers upon the businessman a special responsibility to perform creditably and display a favorable image. Some argue that power requires responsibility and that the businessman must accept new and enlarged responsibilities today because prosperity has enormously augmented his power. Still others maintain that the businessman is today relatively free from the restrictions which competition once imposed and that he must therefore learn to regulate his own behavior if he wishes to avoid regulation by the government.

This last view has been officially endorsed in the highest Washington circles. Presidents Eisenhower, Kennedy, and Johnson have all maintained that the recognition and assumption by businessmen of their social responsibilities is a preferred alternative to government regulation. As a matter of policy, businessmen should be left free to buy, produce, and sell; but the price which society demands for this freedom is the subordination of private gain to public welfare. The social responsibility of businessmen has consequently been invoked at one time or another as the cure for such problems as inflation, the balance-of-payments deficit, highway safety, the unemployment created by automation, and water pollution, to mention just a few from a long and apparently growing list.

It must also be remembered that success breeds its own dissatisfactions. In the last twenty years the American economy has responded remarkably well to the demands placed upon it, providing steadily rising incomes, high employment, and the goods and services for vastly expanded public welfare programs, while simultaneously meeting the huge requirements of national defense. The end result has not always been complacency and self-satisfaction, but rather quite often a search for new challenges and for ways of resolving old problems that were once deemed insoluble. The current "war on poverty" and the whole civil rights movement exemplify the way in which standards and expectations rise at least as fast as performance improves.

Perhaps this is why critics are so rarely impressed by the record of the business community, whether in the economic or the ethical realm. "From him to whom much has been given much is required." If fundamental needs have now by and large been met, it is time to be concerned for the quality of American life and for those disagreeable aspects of business practice which had to be overlooked in a less prosperous era. Thus more attention is paid today to such business scandals as the payola cases or the electrical price conspiracy. More acute questions are raised about the inequalities of wealth and power in our society and about the role which businessmen allegedly play in creating and perpetuating them. More people are alarmed by the appearance of the "organization man" or the power of the "hidden persuaders" or the techniques of the "privacy invaders." And so the demand for a greater measure of social responsibility on the part of businessmen has intensified.

CONSENSUS AND CONFUSION

The majority of American businessmen are today willing, even eager to agree that business must recognize and accept its new social responsibilities.[1] The view that the businessman is responsible only to himself and his firm or that the maximization of profits should be the dominant criterion in business decision making is vigorously rejected by leading business spokesmen as outmoded and unrealistic.[2] Businessmen have been important molders and consumers of the growing literature on social responsibility, and they are eager to talk about the subject at trade conventions and special conferences.

But the outcome of all this active interest has not been any clearer conception of just what social responsibility entails. Each symposium on the question begins and ends about where the last one did: with the assertion that businessmen do indeed have social responsibilities and must give them their proper weight in making important decisions.[3] The impression often left is that businessmen need to be converted. But the bulk of the evidence points in another direction: They need to be educated.

No one will deny that some businessmen are scoundrels. At the same time, scoundrels are not ordinarily in attendance at seminars on social responsibility, and in any event no sensible person will hope to eliminate blatantly fraudulent and unscrupulous business practices through exhortations to ethical behavior. It is only the ethical businessman who is listening, the businessman already convinced that it is his duty to act in accord with the welfare of society. The obvious need, therefore, is for education, not conversion.

What kind of education? To what body of truth should the businessman be introduced? How are his social responsibilities to be discerned? What are they?

These questions have been rendered more urgent by our apparent decision to construct public policy upon the assumption that businessmen can and will be socially responsible. The President has told businessmen that price controls or a tax increase can be avoided in periods of inflationary pressure if they will make responsible pricing decisions. The Secretary of the Treasury has informed bankers that a tighter monetary policy can be avoided if they will consider the national interest in extending loans. Corporations investing abroad have been warned officially that they can expect controls on capital exports unless they adjust their overseas investment programs to take account of the national interest. But it is precisely at these points that the fatal ambiguity of the underlying concept has been revealed. After the rhetoric has waned and the time arrives for translating assurances of cooperation into concrete decisions, businessmen simply do not agree with government officials or even among themselves on just what social responsibility requires.

We all think that we know what social responsibility means until we begin to make practical use of the concept. Then its extraordinary ambiguity emerges. But by that time it is often too late. Positions have been taken and hostages given. Then there is rarely the mood or the audience for a dispassionate analysis of what we are saying and what we finally intend.

When a question is repeatedly asked but never satisfactorily answered, we should begin to suspect that the question harbors some confusion. That is the principal thesis of this book. The businessman's social responsibility is both an economic and an ethical notion. But neither economics nor ethics is so simple a subject as we have imagined.

Notes to Chapter I.

[1] A skeptic or a cynic might question this, of course. What businessmen say, especially for public consumption, does not necessarily conform to what they believe. But numerous personal conversations and even debates with businessmen on this subject have convinced the writer that if businessmen are deceiving anyone, they are deceiving themselves first of all.

[2] Raymond C. Baumhart, "How Ethical Are Businessmen?" *Harvard Business Review* (July–August, 1961), pp. 8, 10. For a critical survey of some of the pronouncements made on this topic by leading business spokesmen, see Robert L. Heilbroner, "The View from the Top," in Earl F. Cheit (ed.), *The Business Establishment* (John Wiley & Sons, Inc., New York, 1964).

[3] It would be invidious to single out particular examples. But even the participants in such symposia have begun to say out loud what many must have long been thinking: The emperor has no clothes.

II.

Economics and the Public Good

T he role of social responsibility in an economic system
was briefly discussed by Adam Smith in *Wealth of Nations*. His comments are worth recalling:

> Man has almost constant occasion for the help of his brethren, and it is vain for him to expect it from their benevolence only. He will be more likely to prevail if he can interest their self-love in his favour, and shew them that it is for their own advantage to do for him what he requires of them. . . . It is not from the benevolence of the butcher, the brewer, or the baker, that we expect our dinner, but from their regard to their own interest. We address ourselves, not to their humanity but to their self-love, and never talk to them of our own necessities but of their advantages.[1]

> Every individual is continually exerting himself to find out the most advantageous employment for whatever capital he can command. It is his own advantage, indeed, and not that

of the society, which he has in view. But the study of his own advantage naturally, or rather necessarily leads him to prefer that employment which is most advantageous to the society.[2] He generally, indeed, neither intends to promote the public interest, nor knows how much he is promoting it. . . . he intends only his own gain, and he is in this, as in many other cases, led by an invisible hand to promote an end which was no part of his intention. Nor is it always the worse for the society that it was no part of it. By pursuing his own interest he frequently promotes that of the society more effectually than when he really intends to promote it. I have never known much good done by those who affected to trade for the public good.[3]

If Adam Smith was right, we are wasting our time attempting to define the social responsibilities of businessmen. The public good will be promoted most effectively when each businessman assiduously pursues his own advantage. But the majority verdict today is that Smith was wrong; while his argument may contain an element of truth (and few would deny this), it is no longer possible to believe that the public good will by some mysterious alchemy emerge from universal selfishness.

Why is Smith's view no longer accepted, if indeed it ever was? Where was he misled? What did his argument leave out?

The most common way of refuting Smith's argument really misses the point and cannot be called a refutation at all. That "invisible hand" (the phrase occurs but once in *Wealth of Nations*) is only a metaphor; Smith cannot be refuted by an attack upon invisible hands, natural laws, or deistic assumptions, any more than we can refute the "law of gravity" by proving that no legislature ever passed it. The invisible hand and the law of gravity both claim to summarize observable phenomena, things whose operation can be discerned in the real world whatever the name by which we choose to speak of them. The question here is not whether an invisible

hand exists but whether the pursuit of private gain does in
fact promote the public good. Smith was not talking theology
or metaphysics, but economics.

His argument is now generally recognized as deficient
in several ways. But economists have refined that argument in
the intervening years, and it is possible to state with considerable precision the premises from which Smith's conclusion
does in fact follow.

DEFINING THE PUBLIC GOOD

It follows, first of all, from a particular definition of *public
good*, a definition which equates public good and the optimal
allocation of economic resources. An *optimal resource allocation* is in turn defined as an allocation which maximizes the
value of total output. Put another way, resources are opti-
mally allocated when the value of total output could not be
increased by using resources in any alternative way.

A large part of economic theory is simply an elaboration
of the conditions required for such an allocation of resources.
The complicated set of marginal equalities which must be
satisfied will be familiar to all economists and unintelligible to
most others, so their precise statement has been assigned to a
note.[4] The significant proposition, which can be grasped without any formal training in economic theory, is that these equalities will be satisfied in an economic system that conforms to
the following specifications:

1. The prices of all inputs and outputs are market-clearing
prices (quantity demanded equals quantity supplied).
2. All buyers and sellers face the same prices, and none has
the power to alter them.
3. All buyers and sellers are free to take advantage of these
prices.
4. Every buyer and seller maximizes his net advantage.

The first three conditions specify what the economist calls *pure competition*. The last postulates utility maximization by consumers and profit maximization by business firms. The argument can be roughly summarized as follows: The public good is achieved when everyone seeks to maximize his own advantage under conditions of pure competition.

To claim, then, that Adam Smith's judgment on this issue is not valid today is to claim either that optimal resource allocation cannot be identified with the public good or that the economic system is not actually competitive—or both.

THE CRUCIAL QUESTION

If all of this seems somewhat abstract, it is nonetheless an essential preliminary to any intelligent discussion of the issue. Social responsibility on the part of businessmen is an economic concept, whatever else it is, and wherever it is discussed some kind of economic analysis is presupposed. Businessmen's decisions are made and will inevitably be made in the light of economic facts, facts of supply and demand, and they will have economic consequences, consequences for the allocation of resources. These facts and consequences are not matters of secondary importance which can safely be relegated to discussion in an appendix. They are at the heart of what we are talking about, whether we realize it or not, when we begin to discuss the businessman's social responsibility. The businessman plays a dominant role in the organization and use of society's economic resources. When therefore we propose to him new rules of behavior, we are in fact recommending a different use of those resources; and it is essential that we perceive the consequences of what we recommend. Any discussion of the businessman's social responsibility which does not begin with economic analysis is sound and fury, signifying nothing at best, creating confusion at worst.

The crucial questions, then, are these:

1. Is the American economy adequately competitive today? Or is monopoly power too important a feature of the contemporary American scene for us reasonably to expect that profit maximization by businessmen will lead to the optimal allocation of resources?

2. What has been ignored when we equate the public good with the optimal allocation of resources? In what major respects is this definition deficient?

THE LIMITATIONS OF ECONOMICS

"Optimal" is a technical word in this context and cannot uncritically be assumed to mean "best." Economists have themselves taken pains to point out why and how an optimal resource allocation (in the technical sense) can differ from a socially most advantageous allocation.

In the first place and most importantly, that allocation which will be optimal in any society depends upon the initial distribution of wealth. The consumer choices which are expressed in the market and which direct the employment of resources depend upon the wealth as well as the personal preferences of each consumer. For reasons both biological and social, wealth is not equally—and some would say not equitably—distributed. A different distribution, one more in line, let us say, with a particular notion of equitability, would result in a different allocation of economic resources and one quite possibly closer to the preferences of a majority.

Secondly, the logical demonstration that utility and profit maximization leads inexorably to an optimal allocation under competitive conditions implicitly assumes that there are no social revenues or social costs which diverge significantly from private revenues and costs. It is obvious that this condition is not fully satisfied in any actual economic system. Factories inflict smoke, dirt, noise, and congestion upon the neighborhood; these are very real costs, but they are not borne by the owners of the factory. This understatement of costs results in the overemployment of resources. Similarly, the grass seed, peat moss, and perspiration which one home-owner invests in his lawn usually yields a return greater than the increase in his own satisfaction; his neighbors also derive "revenue" from his activity. Any understatement of revenue because of "neighborhood benefits" will have as its consequence the underemployment of resources. In sum, to the extent that market prices fail to take account of *all* costs and benefits, the pursuit of individual advantage under competitive conditions need not result in the best possible allocation of resources.

These two qualifications are the ones that economists have usually stressed. But infinite variations can be rung on these themes. It has been objected that efficiency in resource use is one good among others, that it often conflicts with other goods, and that social welfare will sometimes require the sacrifice of efficiency for the sake of a competing good. This is really a version of the second argument above. An interesting version of this version alleges that competition is in itself evil because it manifests or encourages selfishness; for those attracted by this argument, there is a strong prima facie case against identifying an optimal allocation of resources with the public good.

WHAT ARE WE AFTER?

But it is not enough merely to show that the public good *could* require an allocation of resources different from what would result in a system of pure competition. *Does* it? In what respects? Why? And the crucial question: What system for organizing economic activity and controlling economic decisions will lead to a closer approximation of the public good?

It is usually easy to demonstrate that an existing system is not perfect. But the imperfections of one system do not prove the superiority of any alternative. It would be unnecessary to say this if we were not all so much in the habit of "proving B by disproving A." Airplanes sometimes crash; that does not prove that automobiles are safer. The pursuit of private advantage creates problems; that does not prove that the acceptance by businessmen of certain social responsibilities will create fewer or less grave problems.

Part of the task before us will be to decide how businessmen do behave today and what the consequences are. But we shall also have to ask what the consequences would be if they began in wholesale fashion to "trade for the public good."

Notes to Chapter II.

[1] Adam Smith, *Wealth of Nations* (Modern Library, Inc., New York, 1937), p. 14.

[2] *Ibid.*, p. 421.

[3] *Ibid.*, p. 423.

[4] Paul Samuelson has stated them most succinctly: "Between any two variables, the marginal rates of substitution must be (subjectively) equal for all individuals, and (technically) equal for all alternative processes, with the common technical and subjective ratios being equivalent." "Comment," in Bernard F. Haley (ed.), *A Survey of Contemporary Economics,* vol. II (Richard D. Irwin, Inc., Homewood, Ill., 1952), p. 38.

III.

The Meaning and Functions of Business

Business" is an exceptionally comprehensive term, so comprehensive, it seems, that we have been compelled to substitute an "i" to distinguish it from mere busy-ness. What do we mean by "business"? What is it that the businessman does?

"Business is what the businessman does, and a businessman is a man engaged in business." That sort of definition is often useful in getting us over unimportant preliminaries and into the meat of an issue. But in this case a good deal of meat may cling to the not-so-bare bones of a definition.

The *businessman* has often been defined as one concerned with the material side of life, with the ordinary affairs of life, or with those things that have a monetary value. These defitions have one thing in common besides their vagueness and inaccuracy: they are all subtly demeaning. The connotation of "material" is grubby, uncultured; "ordinary" means ordinary, not exciting, not important; and the things that have a monetary value are in common thought the things that do not have "ultimate" value. Not everyone who employs these definitions intends these connotations; but they are always lurking, and they have a way of coloring our conception of business and the businessman.

"A man who knows the price of everything and the value of nothing" was Oscar Wilde's definition of a cynic, not of a businessman. Yet it manages to capture the flavor of what we mean when we speak of the businessman as a businessman. Individual businessmen, in their personal lives, are frequently noble, generous, and cultivated. But the businessman *qua* businessman . . . There are many ways in which people finish that sentence, but a large percentage of them amount to ". . . is concerned with price, not value."

WHAT'S IN A NAME?

Such an attitude is not confined to business critics, but is often found among businessmen themselves. One of the best examples is in a book, *Business and Society*, by the dean of a business school, a book that has been widely heralded in the business press. Dean Joseph McGuire defines business as "a way of life wherein materialistic wants are satisfied. . . . nearly everything is business that in some way satisfies materialistic human wants." [1]

Dean McGuire makes his meaning even clearer when he continues:

> Business . . . *is* a way of life. In the United States, in fact, it may be said that business is *the* way of life. . . . business is deeply imbedded in our American society.
>
> People of other nations, for example, think of the United States as a materialistic country. By this, they mean that the

"big" question for our people is not "Is it good?" or (as the French say) "Is it bad?" Rather, our "big" question seems to them to be "What's in it for me?" Furthermore, they are probably not often wrong in this assumption. As we look about us, for example, we observe that many of our students are in college not to obtain an education, but to get grades—to get a degree, a "union card" as some of them term it. Our books are written not to last through the ages and to contain that modicum of basic truth or wisdom or beauty, but to become immediate best sellers. As such, modern authors often have found it more profitable to appeal to the baser nature of man than to emphasize the eternal verities. Somehow, too, I can't imagine Pollack or de Kooning or any of the other modern abstract American artists holding the attention of a wide circle of art fanciers in the same way that Rembrandt or Goya have over the centuries. Even our songs today have little musical or aesthetic value: They are written not because they are lovely, but because the guttural groans and grunts of the vocalists appeal to teen-agers, and thus are "money makers." It seems, then, that almost anything we mention in our American society has some materialistic—business—tinge.[2]

Here is a remarkable example of the associations and connotations to which we have referred. Business is associated with materialism, amorality, selfishness, academic time-serving, pornography(?), and cultural impoverishment. Small wonder if the businessman sometimes feels defensive.

The remarkable thing about all these denotations and connotations is that they really have no discernible connection with business. Business is *not* a matter of satisfying materialistic human wants but of satisfying *any* human wants— for pork chops, classical records, museums, or this book. True, business strives to satisfy primarily those wants to which a price tag can be attached. But the obvious explanation is that only exchangeable values can in any systematic way be "provided for," and only exchangeable values have price tags. Does the desire for a healthy heart become a materialistic want the moment science learns to build artificial hearts and someone starts to produce and sell them? Is my desire to visit the art gallery materialistic if an admission is charged? In one sense *all* human wants are materialistic, from the desire to be loved to the urge to drive a sports car. And viewed in another way *no* human want is materialistic, but only the means through which a want is satisfied.

But perhaps the word "materialism" is a misnomer. When Dean McGuire says that we are a materialistic country because our "big question" is "What's in it for me?" he seems to suggest that "materialistic" really means selfish. If we accept this definition, it is still not easy to see the connection between business and materialism. Are businessmen peculiarly selfish? Or are the human desires that business serves selfish in some unique way? Neither proposition holds up under examination.

The desire for monetary wealth is not in itself selfish. Wealth confers the power to endow monasteries, purchase life insurance, engage in conspicuous consumption, or do thousands of other things that may or may not express a selfish attitude. In fact, the refusal to accumulate monetary wealth could just as well be selfish, as when a man chooses idleness in preference to supporting his family.

But Dean McGuire's illustrations of a selfish attitude suggest that it is not really selfishness that he is talking about, either. It is rather poor taste, a narrow attitude toward life, an inability to appreciate music, painting, and ideas. But by this time we have got quite far from business as a way of life. Is there any connection at all between business and the cultural impoverishment which allegedly characterizes the United States? The argument has drifted into a sea of nebulous and highly debatable assertions. There is a large market in this country for classical music as well as the grunt-and-groan variety; good books are written as well as sordid ones; if Pollack and de Kooning do not rank with Rembrandt and Goya, how many painters in other, less "business-oriented" cultures do? And what does any of this have to do finally with business?

The point of all this is not to reprimand Dean McGuire but to illustrate the strange and unwarranted hostility that so many Americans entertain toward the concept of business. Somehow we have got into the habit of saying "business-like" when we mean selfish, sordid, or provincial. The unfortunate consequences of this careless way of thinking and speaking are becoming serious.

One consequence is the number of college students who in recent years have come to regard careers in business as uninteresting and even dehumanizing; for the creative and talented person, business is only the last resort. Many of those already in business wonder, too, whether life is not passing them by, whether they may not have sold their birthrights for a mess of pottage. The rhetoric of self-glorification that pours so profusely from business apologists is, like most boasting, more indicative of an inferiority complex than of genuine pride. It is beginning to look as if the businessman himself has lost confidence in the meaning of what he is doing.

It is high time, therefore, to look again at what we mean by business and what it is that the businessman does.

THE BUSINESSMAN AS ARCHITECT

The business sector of society is that sector in which men are occupied with the organization of resources for the satisfaction of human wants. In a very true and important sense, this includes *all of life.* Insofar as we live "rationally," we strive to organize available resources (time, love, and psychic energy, as well as bricks, steel, land, and labor) to secure a maximum of satisfaction. (We do not, of course, always live "rationally" in this sense, and it would be "irrational" to do so. There is a marginal utility from not bothering about marginal utility.) Rationality here means the use of means in a manner appropriate to the ends chosen. The businessman, as it turns out, is society's principal architect of rationality; and business finally is the rational aspect of society.

It is important to note that the word "rational" is being used in a restricted but nonetheless extremely broad sense. Its meaning here comes very close to "logical." The task of business is to organize resources logically.

All of us have goals, values, desires—ends to be pursued. The limitations on our ability to attain our ends, individually or jointly, can best be summarized as a scarcity of resources. The possibilities that are contained in available resources will be fully realized only if those resources are combined and employed logically. Society looks primarily to business to achieve logic, rationality, and efficiency in the deployment of its resources. Businessmen form the group in society principally charged with the responsibility for so ordering available resources that a maximum of what is desired can be attained.

There is nothing grubby, materialistic, selfish, unimportant, or in any way demeaning about this task. The more successfully the businessman fulfills this assignment, the more possibilities he opens up for his society. It may well occur that these possibilities will be squandered in idiotic entertainments and chrome-plated gadgets; but they may also be enjoyed in the form of meaningful education, broadening travel, openhanded charity, and creative leisure.

The mere possibility will not create great men or a good society. But nothing great or good will be achieved in the absence of possibility.

THE BUSINESSMAN AS ARTIST

The unifying concept in the world of business is not materialism or selfishness at all, but *economy*. And economy is a value. It has nothing to do with the justly derided "economic man," who turns out upon inspection to be miserly or just silly rather than economical. In its deepest meaning, economy is part of the sense of proportion, of the fitness of things, which is an ideal of all human activity.

An aesthetically refined person will be repelled by the interior of a downtown "movie palace" because it is "gross" and "ostentatious." He will conclude that the designer had no respect for his materials or their function: that he failed to practice economy.

In any great work of art, there is nothing wasted, nothing superfluous; it is economical. Shakespeare could have written: "The inevitable human tendency to deliberate before acting and to ponder the consequences of an action frequently deters us from making and implementing a vital decision." But Shakespeare was an economizer and wrote: "Conscience doth make cowards of us all."

Art is not just a matter of economy, of course, and the economical use of means is not enough for the achievement of great ends. But economy is intimately related to art, and economy is without question a value in and of itself.

We shall return to this theme later on to see if it can make any contribution toward resolving the apparent crisis of confidence among contemporary businessmen. This lengthy and somewhat abstract argument about the meaning of words and concepts has been introduced here because we are trying to grasp the nature of the businessman's social responsibilities. The conclusion of our argument is that the businessman's primary and overriding responsibility is to use the resources of society in the most economical way.

Any argument which maintains that this is some kind of secondary responsibility rests upon a fundamental confusion. Economy opens possibilities; we cannot conceive of an argument which would make of economy anything but an unqualified good. What use is made of these possibilities or for what purposes people employ the enhanced freedom and power which economy confers is an important question; but it is an entirely separate one.

Notes to Chapter III.

[1] Joseph W. McGuire, *Business and Society* (McGraw-Hill Book Company, New York, 1963), pp. 29–30. In fairness to McGuire it must be pointed out that he himself finds his definition rather inadequate. But he does not indicate why it is inadequate, and he does, after all, put it forward as a useful definition.

[2] *Ibid.*, pp. 30–31.

IV.

The Economics of Profit Maximization

T he social responsibility of the businessman is to play his part in achieving an optimal allocation of society's resources. The public good, broadly conceived, certainly includes more than this; but it requires no more than this of the businessman as a businessman. In this chapter we shall attempt to show that the demand for something more easily becomes a demand for something less.

Some who would accept this as an abstract definition of the businessman's social responsibilities will also maintain that it provides only a formal definition. They would say that this definition leaves the businessman still in the dark as to what he ought to do in any given situation, what practical criteria he should use in making decisions, and what weights he should assign to the various alternatives before him. But such a notion is mistaken. *Acceptance of this responsibility by the businessman entails an obligation to maximize the profits of his enterprise.* What this obligation will require in any situation depends, of course, upon the businessman's total assessment of that situation. But the criterion for decision is clear: the maximization of profits.

A FALSE DICHOTOMY

The argument of the preceding chapter should have made clear that efficiency in the use of society's resources is a goal both important and humane. When John Maynard Keynes referred to economists as "the keepers of the possibility of civilization," he was saying something very much like what we have asserted about the businessman. The efficient use of resources opens up possibilities—all kinds of possibilities. If we fail to make good use of these possibilities, that is no more the fault of the businessman than it is the fault of every other member of society. It is illegitimate to contend that humanist goals must take precedence over economic goals, and thereby deprecate the importance of economic efficiency. Economic efficiency is the servant of humanist aspirations and not their rival, and if we fail to achieve a worthwhile civilization the fault lies with all of us, not with those who have created the possibility.[1]

Many people will react negatively to the suggestion that businessmen should concentrate on profit maximization because they have attached all sorts of sordid connotations to the concept of profit maximization. Their image of the profit maximizer is that of a squalid man of mean tastes and shriveled soul who would foreclose his mother's mortgage were she a day delinquent. This is nonsensical and has nothing to do with the process of maximizing profits.

To maximize profits, the businessman continues to employ

inputs or resources in minimum-cost combinations until the anticipated value to his enterprise of their marginal product no longer exceeds the price he must pay to obtain them. This rule describes the way businessmen do by and large behave, subject, of course, to all the guesses and uncertainties characteristic of a complex and changing world. The essence of good business management is the accurate application of this rule. And the more accurately and consistently it is applied, the closer will we come to an optimal allocation of resources.

Much misunderstanding will be avoided if we note at once that this is proposed as a rule for making business decisions, not as a philosophy of life. Most of the time the businessman will behave the way everyone else does: in accord with habit, convention, an innate sense of propriety, or ordinary human empathy. When his secretary drops a file folder he will pick it up without calculating the potential profit; he will have the office water cooler repaired without reflection; he will automatically go to lunch at noon. Any businessman who came to believe that profit maximization is a philosophy of life and who tried never to act except upon careful calculations of expected costs and revenue would be a candidate for analysis.

When we call upon the businessman to fulfill his social responsibilities we are asking him to make important decisions in light of the obligations which he owes to society. And these are the decisions which should be made with maximum anticipated profit as the criterion. For in this way the businessman most effectively promotes the optimal allocation of resources. He will not and should not be expected to do it for this reason; he will be seeking "his own advantage, indeed, and not that of the society." But so much the better. This gives him an incentive, constant and pervasive, to perform his social duty carefully and well.

BENEVOLENCE AND BEGGARS

Adam Smith was a shrewd guide in this matter. "Man has almost constant occasion for the help of his brethren," he observed, "and it is vain for him to expect it from their benevolence only." It may not always be vain; but it is highly uncertain; and it is frequently degrading.

If our dinner depended upon the benevolence of the butcher, we would go hungry when the butcher was too tired to open the shop, or more interested in watching a baseball game than in preparing his weekly order, or just plain cantankerous, or even hostile to our political or religious views.

A college professor is typically far less eager to aid a student whom he knows well than a gasoline station attendant is to serve a motorist whom he has never seen before. Adam Smith had some pungent observations to make on this phenomenon:

> The teacher is prohibited from receiving any honorary or fee from his pupils, and his salary constitutes the whole of the revenue which he derives from his office. His interest is, in this case, set as directly in opposition to his duty as it is possible to set it. It is the interest of every man to live as much at his ease as he can; and if his emoluments are to be precisely the same, whether he does, or does not perform some very laborious duty, it is . . . his interest . . . to neglect it. . . . If he is naturally active and a lover of labour, it is his interest to employ that activity in any way, from which he can derive some advantage, rather than in the performance of his duty, from which he can derive none.[2]

The point is not that college professors are an ignoble breed, but rather that service is almost always surer and better when there is an incentive to perform well.

Perhaps it would be a finer world if people were not this way, but the world we have is the one in which we must live. And there is something dehumanizing—this is the neglected other side of the coin—about being *compelled* to rely upon the benevolence of others. How far will he be willing to go? How much can we reasonably ask? What unstated obligations are we incurring? A world in which everyone was *compelled* to rely upon the benevolence of others would be a world of beggars. For most of us that is not a satisfactory human ideal.

THE ETHICS OF COMPETITION

But what of the morality of an economic system founded upon selfishness? This objection, so troublesome to many for whom love is the basic virtue and selfishness its direct opposite, must be rejected before it can be answered. The system we are talking about is not founded upon selfishness but upon profit maximization. A few examples should make it clear that the two are not identical.

A businessman maximizes the profits of his firm and keeps a bare subsistence income for himself, donating the remainder to charity. How is he selfish?

A man volunteers to serve without pay as the business manager of an orphanage. He does the best job he can by striving to maximize profits. (A nonprofit organization that is efficiently run maximizes profits, too.) Is this selfish?

If these examples seem farfetched, imagine the "worst" sort of case. A man owning and operating his own business makes every important decision solely on the basis of the contribution it will make to his net income. Is he selfish? Perhaps. How are we to tell—assuming that we must pass moral judgment upon him? Obviously by examining what he does with that income, and with his time, and with all his other capacities and powers. If he neglects his family, acknowledges no human obligations, and counts any amount of suffering by others as less important than his own small comforts, he is a selfish man. But any connection between this and his profit-maximizing decisions as a businessman is accidental.

Economy is a value, a value in itself and an instrumental value. Volumes of futile discussion could be avoided if the truth of this proposition were finally appreciated. No understanding person claims that economy is enough. It is not a sufficient condition, but it is a necessary condition for a society rich in humane possibilities.

That is why we are in effect asking the businessman to shirk his responsibilities when we ask him to forgo maximum profits. We manage to persuade ourselves that we are really demanding socially desirable behavior by ignoring most of the consequences of what we ask. This self-delusion works because the unintended consequences are often difficult to trace while the intended consequence is immediate and apparent.

MANY A SLIP 'TWIXT CUP AND LIP

The argument that failure to maximize profits interferes with resource allocation is perhaps too "abstract" to convince anyone except economists and those already persuaded. This would be a powerful advertisement for more courses in economic principles were it not for the scandalous fact—widely acknowledged among economists—that most students who take such a course carry little away. We shall therefore take the next best alternative and, at the risk of pedanticism, attempt to illustrate the central proposition.

Consider the following situation. Rumors of frost damage to the coffee crop are heard. Very quickly and long before the frost has had any impact on supply, the price of coffee rises in the grocery stores. Why does the price rise? The usual answer is "profiteering," and that is a correct answer if by profiteering we mean profit maximization and not "merciless exploitation."

The rumor of frost damage causes processors and jobbers holding stocks of coffee to anticipate a future price higher than they originally expected. Their response is to hold back some of the current supply for sale later at a higher price. But with current demand undiminished (or even increased through housewives' own anticipation of higher prices later) the market-clearing price must rise.

The higher current price alters the decisions of both suppliers and consumers. A little more coffee is released for current consumption, and housewives are deterred somewhat in their purchases by the higher price. Prices and sales are shifting because people are "profiteering"; but in the process available resources are being allocated in a more rational fashion. Coffee is being shifted through time from a period of relative abundance to a period of relative scarcity.

What would occur if a local grocer decided that his social responsibility required him to keep his price at its present level? He would find his coffee stocks rapidly depleted. He would be a public benefactor only until his stocks were exhausted; after that he would be the irritating phenomenon of a grocer with no coffee on his shelves. If he tried then to replenish his stocks, he would find out that the cost had gone up and he was now compelled to raise his price. Unless all other merchants had experienced a similar attack of social responsibility! Then he would find that the price of coffee had climbed out of sight.

A price is income to a seller and cost to a buyer. But more importantly, price is a rationing device, a device whereby resources are allocated. Higher prices discourage buyers and encourage sellers; lower prices have the reverse effect. But this assumes that at least some buyers and sellers are trying to maximize profits (or "utility," in the case of housewives).

Even that worst of business villains, the "profiteering speculator," promotes the advantage of society when he tries to maximize his profits. For he causes resources to be allocated differently over time, from a period of feast to one of famine, and thereby alleviates the famine. Unless alternating feast and famine is regarded as better than a steadier flow of any commodity, the speculator performs a public service.

THE SHORTAGE OF COPPER

In recent years a growing demand for copper has been accompanied by a less than proportionate increase in copper production. The consequence (at this writing) is a serious copper shortage. Copper users must stand in line and then content themselves with less copper than they hoped for and are willing to buy. During this same time American copper producers have been urged (some would say "compelled") by the Federal government to refrain in the public interest from raising their prices. There can be no doubt that they want to raise prices, and little doubt that their motive is an increase in profits. But profit maximization and social responsibility allegedly come into conflict here, and the copper producers have been induced to place their social responsibilities ahead of profit considerations.

Has the public interest been served? In a period of increasing copper scarcity, the public interest requires expanded production and economy in consumption. A higher price would have promoted both. It would have made profitable the employment of more resources in the search for and extraction of copper ore. It would have transformed some copper-containing rocks into "ore." And it would have encouraged among buyers a greater use of copper substitutes.

Buyers unable to obtain copper during the current shortage have been *forced* to employ substitutes: other metals; less copper in certain products; curtailment or discontinuance of the production of some items; higher product prices, which in turn discourage purchases. But the way in which this has come about is not consistent with optimal resource allocation.

When buyers are compelled to bid against one another for a commodity in short supply and the price rises, the available stock tends to flow to those for whom it is the most valuable—because they are willing to bid the highest. And this is what society wants of any scarce commodity: its employment first of all in those uses where its value is greatest. The least valuable uses are the ones that should be suspended first in a period of increasing scarcity.

When the price is not allowed to rise, rationing occurs on another basis, such as first-come-first-served or some form of favoritism. But this method of rationing fails to discriminate among users on the basis of value and would be consistent with optimal resource use only by accident.[3]

Government officials may have had their own reasons for holding down the price of copper, and copper producers have had obvious reasons for yielding to government pressure. But any argument that government pressure would have been unnecessary had copper producers shown more concern for the public interest and less for their own profits is simply mistaken. The pursuit of profits called for a price increase; by the test of optimal resource allocation, the public interest called for the same thing.

WHAT IS THE PUBLIC INTEREST?

Imagine the following purely hypothetical case. The owner of a vacant lot decides to sell. A number of prospective buyers present themselves. They inform the owner of the purposes for which they want the lot, and each is different: an apartment, an office building, a parking lot, a gasoline station, and a grocery store. The owner is free to choose to whom he will sell, and by choosing he implicitly decides upon the use to which the lot will be put. He can throw away his power to choose and simply sell to the highest bidder. But let us say that he is a man with a well-developed sense of social responsibility and wants to make sure that the lot is employed in a manner most beneficial to the community. He places the public good ahead of private gain.

But does he really? The price which each buyer is willing to pay reflects the present capitalized value of that buyer's estimate of the profits which will result from his employment of the lot. A sale to the highest bidder means a sale to that buyer who anticipates the largest profit from ownership. But these anticipations are based upon estimates of future costs and revenue associated with a particular employment of the lot. And these estimates in turn reflect the demand for certain services relative to their availablity in the community. All of which is just a way of saying that each buyer will be willing to pay his estimate of the value to society of employing the lot in the manner he intends.

Suppose the highest bid is submitted by the apartment builder and the seller happens to concur in his estimate that this is indeed the most *profitable* prospective use of the land. He decides nonetheless to sell the land for a parking lot on the contention that a parking lot is a more urgent community need. What does this decision mean except that the seller has opposed his notion of community need to the community's own expression of its needs in the marketplace? He may be able to tell himself for years afterward that he acted in the public interest. But *he* defined the public interest, and he defined it in opposition to the best available evidence as to how the community wanted that lot employed. By forgoing a maximum profit from sale of the lot, the seller interfered with the mechanism through which society attempts to secure an optimum allocation of resources. That is his privilege under a system of private property, but it is a strange notion of social responsibility.

THE STEEL PRICE CONTROVERSY

In April, 1962, the United States Steel Corporation announced a $6 per ton increase in the price of steel. The next day President Kennedy went on television to label the increase "a wholly unjustifiable and irresponsible defiance of the public interest." After a quick review of the crises facing the nation and the sacrifices which some were making, the President declared: "The American people will find it hard, as I do, to accept a situation in which a tiny handful of steel executives whose pursuit of private power and profit exceeds their sense of public responsibility can show such utter contempt for the interest of 185 million Americans." [4]

Why was the steel price increase contrary to the public interest? The President laid down a long list of reasons. It would increase the cost of homes, autos, appliances, and most other items in household use, as well as the cost of machinery and tools to businessmen and farmers. It would handicap efforts to prevent an inflationary spiral from eating up the pensions of older citizens and new gains in purchasing power. It would add 1 billion dollars to the cost of national defense. It would make American goods less competitive in international markets and thus aggravate the balance-of-payments and gold-loss problem. And it would handicap efforts to induce other industries and unions to adopt responsible price and wage policies. "The facts of the matter," the President asserted, "are that there is no justification for an increase in steel prices."

One day after President Kennedy's news conference, Board Chairman Roger Blough of United States Steel defended the price increase. He began by accepting his social responsibilities. The executives of United States Steel were, he said, as deeply concerned with the welfare, the strength, and the vitality of the nation as were those who had criticized their action. They were under the requirement to discharge faithfully their responsibilities to the corporation; but they were at the same time committed fully to discharge their responsibilities to the nation. "The action we have taken," said Mr. Blough, "is designed to meet both these responsibilities."

The argument which followed was a familiar one. The nation's strength depended greatly upon its productive machinery and equipment. A company could keep its portion of the nation's physical assets in good working order only by being profitable. Revenue had to be sufficient to pay employees, other expenses, the tax collector, and shareholders for the use of their resources, with something left over to enlarge and improve physical assets. If machinery and equipment were not kept up to date, there would be no sales, no jobs, no taxes paid, and the nation's balance of payments, gold reserves, and rate of economic growth would all suffer.

WHO WAS RIGHT?

Both sides agreed that prices should be set in accord with the nation's interest. But which party to the dispute was correctly perceiving that interest? Critics of Mr. Blough can argue that his analysis was distorted by self-interest. Critics of President Kennedy can reply that Mr. Blough was much better informed about conditions in the steel industry. The interesting thing is that both contentions ultimately support the same conclusion: The businessman's sense of social responsibility cannot be relied upon to regulate prices in accord with the public interest.

The businessman's analysis will inevitably be distorted by self-interest. This bias is in no way unique to businessmen. We do not allow college students to grade their own examinations, politicians to determine their own qualifications for office, or the manager of the home team to call balls and strikes. No man should be a judge in his own case, not because all men are dishonest and self-seeking, but because interest is always capable of distorting judgment. When the evidence is not perfectly clear and the considerations to be taken into account are numerous and complex, there is no way to prove satisfactorily that a decision was not biased. The appropriate procedure in such circumstances, therefore, is to have the decision made by someone who has no special interest in the outcome. That is why judges sometimes disqualify themselves. That is the sense in conflict-of-interest regulations. It is common sense.

But if Mr. Blough cannot be trusted to define the public interest with respect to steel prices, does it follow that the President of the United States *can?* Here it is not so much a matter of bias as of incompetence. A responsible economic decision must be made on the basis of information about anticipated costs and revenues; the executives of a firm know far more about these matters in their own industry than the President of the United States can possibly know. The public interest will not always require stable or declining prices for one particular firm's product. Prices can be too low, in light of demand, other prices, or resource availabilities, as well as too high. How can anyone reach a decision without an intimate knowledge of the market, the firm, and the industry? The answer is that no one can. Therefore the President of the United States, while qualified by his position to define the public interest in one sense, lacks the competence to determine exactly what the public interest requires in the way of a particular firm's decisions.

Then who *will* care for the public interest?

A question for a question: Who cared for the public interest in the dark days when businessmen allegedly scorned their social responsibilities and government officials supposedly believed that economic decisions were exclusively private matters? The answer, of course, is the market.

THE TEST OF THE MARKET

Mr. Blough might have replied to the President in quite a different way. He might have said: "My dear Mr. President, you fail to see how a market economy works. If we can expand our profits by raising prices, this is evidence that insufficient resources are being allocated to steel production. The higher prices will attract those resources. The only adequate and valid test of our action is the market, and this is the test we propose to try. I know as much about the steel industry as anyone, and I frankly don't have the faintest notion what kind of price for steel is required in the *national* interest. I don't know what a socially responsible price would look like. Therefore we price to maximize our profits. This is the only way we know to serve the public interest. If we abandon the market test, as you would apparently have us do, what possible criteria can we have for mediating among the dozens of conflicting demands made upon us, all of them ostensibly in the public interest? There are demands for higher wages, for higher dividends, for higher prices paid to suppliers, for lower prices to steel consumers, for full employment, for price stability, for more efficient steel production, for more jobs in the steel industry, and so on and on. The mind reels. You just have no idea what you are asking. It is quite true that we have placed 'private power and profit' in the forefront of our thinking; but this is not inconsistent with the public interest. You yourself have asserted that 'price and wage decisions . . . are and ought to be freely and privately made.' Do you understand why? It is not so that businessmen and others may enjoy the freedom of arbitrary choice. We want economic decisions freely and privately made because we maintain that an economy is best governed by decentralized decision making integrated through the market. What is bad about government price-fixing is that it ignores the information and the dictates of the market. The same objection will apply to private price-setting if businessmen take seriously the exhortation to set prices in accord with the national interest. The flaw in each case is the same: The market is ignored."

Mr. Blough did not respond in this fashion. Perhaps he wanted to, but deemed it unwise to read the President a lecture on economic principles. Or, just possibly, Mr. Blough might not have cared to call attention to the market. For the theory of a market economy asserts that private decisions oriented toward maximum profits best serve the public interest when there is substantial competition, and Mr. Blough might not have cared to raise unnecessarily the question of whether the steel industry is adequately competitive.

But this was the real issue. Food prices rose sharply in 1965, from 106.6 in the Consumer Price Index to 110.6, with much more of an effect on the cost of living than the aborted steel price hike could possibly have had. Yet no one accused farmers of failing to price in the public interest, for farmers have no power to do so. The price of agricultural commodities is set by supply and demand, by the market, by the impersonal mechanism through which society directs the economizing process.

CLARIFYING THE ISSUE

There are, then, two possibilities. Either a businessman faces a situation sufficiently competitive so that the market can be relied upon to constrain his decisions, or he does not. In the former case our inquiry is ended. It is unreasonable to demand responsible decisions from one who lacks the power to decide irresponsibly. But what of the latter case? Is this not the far more common situation? Do not most businessmen enjoy a substantial amount of monopoly or oligopoly power, so that they are significantly free from the restraints of the market? This is a crucial question, and one to which we must return.

But we need not answer this question in order to answer the one that preceded it: Shall we urge social responsibility upon those businessmen whom the market does not adequately restrain? The economic argument against doing so is simply that a businessman, even with the best intentions in the world, cannot know what the public interest requires. It is sheer nonsense to suppose, for example, that the public interest always requires lower prices and higher wages. Nor do we improve matters by asking for prices "as low as possible" and wages "as high as possible." For what will be possible depends upon what else we are determined to have. A decision to lower prices is inevitably and simultaneously a decision to alter all sorts of other variables as well, because a price change has consequences: for sales, for profits, for employment; for sales, profits, and employment of other firms; and for the overall allocation of resources.

Professor Ben Lewis has stated the essential proposition succinctly and well:

> Basically, however, the difficulty with the corporate conscience thesis is that, preoccupied with the problem of economic morality, it overlooks the problem of economizing. It is not enough that economic decisions made by corporate managements shall be good in the sense of being selfless rather than selfish, in the sense that managements derive happiness and serenity of conscience from smiles of gratitude bestowed upon them by persons other than their stockholders. To economize is to choose between competing goods. Economic choices can rarely bring smiles without concomitant tears; and lonely consciences hold no formulas for the optimum distribution of smiles and tears in our economy. Once again, with gestures: Economizing is society's job! Economic decisions must be right as society measures right rather than good as benevolent individuals construe goodness. An economy is a mechanism designed to pick up and discharge the wishes of society in the management of its resources; it is not an instrument for the rendering of gracious music by kindly disposed improvisers.[5]

It is true that profit maximization on the basis of market information will yield less desirable results from the standpoint of society the less closely the economy approximates the competitive norm. But the problem then is monopoly or insufficient competition, not profit maximization. Monopoly power introduces a distortion. The monopolist's subsequent refusal to maximize his profits will only introduce an additional distortion. It is certainly *possible* that these two distortions could cancel one another out. But it is highly unlikely, and we have moreover no way of knowing just what kind of benevolent decisions by monopolists will cancel out the distortion which that monopoly power introduces. Nor does the monopolist know!

Of course, if we talk enough about social responsibility, we may manage to convince ourselves that the problem of monopoly power can be ignored. But economic theory provides no grounds for believing that the acceptance by businessmen of their social responsibilities is a reasonable equivalent for a public policy of promoting and maintaining competition.

This is the basic economic case against substituting social responsibility for profit maximization. It is by no means the entire case. For as we shall see subsequently, there is also an ethical and a political case to be made against relying upon social responsibility to control the exercise of social power. But before we can discuss these aspects of the problem we must examine a number of issues over which we have skipped too rapidly.

Notes to Chapter IV.

[1] Such assertions as "people are more important than profits" or "human rights must take precedence over property rights" are variations on this mistaken theme. The argument is mistaken not because the reverse is true but because profits and property have

in themselves *no* importance and *no* rights. They are means to *human* ends, and nothing but confusion is gained when they are weighed against ends. It is people who make and use profits. And property rights are a very important part of the rights of human beings. Any alleged instance of a conflict between property rights and human rights turns out upon closer inspection to be a conflict between particular rights being asserted by different people.

[2] Adam Smith, *Wealth of Nations* (Modern Library, Inc., New York, 1937), pp. 717–18.

[3] The Federal Housing Administration, concerned about the copper shortage, recently urged builders to cooperate by using substitute materials "wherever feasible." But the feasibility of substitution reduces finally to a matter of relative cost. By distorting costs, the government has deprived builders of both the necessary knowledge and the incentive to use copper economically. The exhortation was consequently meaningless.

[4] The opposing statements of President Kennedy and Roger Blough may be read in Edwin Mansfield (ed.), *Monopoly Power and Economic Performance* (W. W. Norton & Company, Inc., New York, 1964), pp. 87–94.

[5] Ben W. Lewis, "Economics by Admonition," *American Economic Review,* vol. 49, no. 2 (May, 1959), p. 395.

V.

Ethical Codes: A Blind Alley

I f a reader wished to caricature the argument thus far, he
could say we have been maintaining that ethics and
morality should play no part in the making of business decisions. But this would indeed be a caricature and one far
from accurate. Ethics and morality do play a part in the making of such decisions, they will undoubtedly continue to do
so, and we can be grateful that such is the case. If this appears to contradict what has just been said, an important
distinction has not been noticed: We have argued against *extending* the role which ethics and morality play in the organization of economic life. This is a crucial difference.

THE ACTUAL ROLE OF ETHICS

Economic life in our society rests much more than we ordinarily recognize upon the assumption of "upright" behavior.

Grocery stores assume that most of their customers are not shoplifters, consumer credit departments assume that most of those who buy on the installment plan are not welchers, even the wary customer typically imputes credibility to the bulk of a salesman's claims, and businessmen ordinarily take for granted that a man will be bound by his word. If we could not make these assumptions, economic life would be far more encrusted with red tape, it would flow much less smoothly, and the market would indeed be a sordid place. How much we do in fact rely upon simple trust is best shown by those cases where the trust proves unfounded. The notorious salad oil swindle of Anthony De Angelis is a prime illustration. Banks and other lenders accepted fraudulent warehouse receipts as security for huge loans less critically than they would have examined a $25 personal check.[1] Here they may have overstepped the line between trust and gullibility. But the case illustrates the important and probably indispensable role that confidence in others does play in the smooth functioning of an economic system.

The fact that most businessmen and consumers have relatively high standards of integrity is something for which we can be grateful. It is surely nothing that we wish to change. But neither is it a support upon which we should lean too hard. A useful cane will be broken if it is made to bear excessive weight. And a cane cannot be relied upon to do the work of a pair of crutches.

WHAT ETHICS CANNOT DO

The standards of ordinary behavior are the product of mores, habits, conventions, prudential rules, and ethical principles, derived from religion, history, experience, and the whole process of socialization. They could never be adequately codified because they are too diverse, ambiguous, even inconsistent, and in any event are continually undergoing transformation.

It is like the perception of colors: No one can say just what it is, but we can talk about it, and all but the blind are grateful for it.

A fundamental difficulty with trying to extend ethical standards as instruments of social control is that no one knows just what it is we are trying to extend. It is easy enough to say that businessmen should be more ethical; but what does this mean? Even if we were to agree that it means something relatively specific, like adherence to the golden rule, this would still not be specific enough. Millions of people will assent to the golden rule and yet differ sharply on what constitutes ethical behavior in a given situation.

It sometimes seems that no amount of experience to the contrary will shake our faith in the effectiveness of laying down explicit ethical rules. We want "good" behavior, and we believe against all the evidence that the formulation of ethical codes will contribute significantly to that end. A good part of the contemporary confusion about the businessman's social responsibilities begins right here.

THE INTEREST IN CODES

A number of thoughtful writers, after assessing the ethics of business today, have concluded that ethical codes, drafted perhaps on an industry basis, are a partial solution to the problems they detect.[2] Let us therefore examine business codes of ethics, in practice and in theory, to see what lessons they contain.

Any ethical code will have to come down somewhere between too specific and too general. Our conclusion can be stated in advance: There is no such place. Any code of ethics for business will become too general before it has stopped being too specific; it will be too vague to be of practical use while it is still too detailed and controversial to be acceptable.

This is a hard saying. It condemns in advance all attempts to draft such codes as irrelevant, however well intentioned. Worse than that, we shall suggest that the drafting is not always well intentioned, a fact which may go far to explain why businessmen persist in an "irrelevant" activity.

Concrete examples are best. We have selected, almost at random, the "Code of Ethics" of a Western retail jewelers' association, drawn up with the advice and assistance of the local better business bureau.

Code of Ethics

1. Serve the public with honest values.
2. Tell the truth about what is offered.
3. Tell the truth in a forthright manner so its significance can be understood by the trusting as well as the analytical.
4. Tell customers what they want to know—what they have a right to know and ought to know—about what is offered so that they may buy wisely and obtain the maximum satisfaction from their purchases.
5. Be prepared and willing to make good as promised and without quibble on any guarantee offered.
6. Be sure that the normal use of merchandise or services offered will not be hazardous to public health or life.
7. Reveal material facts, the deceptive concealment of which might cause consumers to be misled.
8. Advertise and sell merchandise or service on its merits and refrain from attacking your competitors or reflecting unfairly upon their products, services, or methods of doing business.
9. If testimonials are used, use only those of competent witnesses who are sincere and honest in what they say about what you sell.
10. Avoid all tricky devices and schemes such as deceitful trade-in allowances, fictitious list prices, false and exaggerated comparative prices, bait advertising, misleading free offers, fake sales, and similar practices which prey upon human ignorance and gullibility.[3]

The code, which is fairly representative, presents such a tempting target for cynical sniping that it is hard to decide where to begin. Number 1 is so vague that we must treat it as purely introductory. Number 2 gets on with the task. But number 3 effectively undermines number 2 by pointing out that truth is a slippery concept. Number 4 finally says something. But does it mean what it says, and does it say what it means? One of the most important pieces of information that a customer would like to have is the percentage markup on the gold wedding band which he is considering. He knows that posted retail prices on such items are customarily far above the cost of the goods to the jeweler, and he knows that if forced to choose between a substantial discount and loss of the sale the jeweler would prefer to grant the discount. A small profit on the item is better than no profit, and the jeweler knows that a discount granted one customer will probably not have to be extended to others. So a bargaining situation exists: There is some price above which the customer will not go, some price below which the retailer will not go. Each is very eager to discover the other's limit. Should the jeweler now put himself at a strategic disadvantage by revealing the wholesale price of the item and thus, implicitly, the limit to which he can be pushed? Turn the question around. Would the customer be obliged to tip his hand by giving an honest answer to the jeweler's quiet "How much were you intending to pay"? If the latter answer is no, why should the former be yes? But the code covers the jeweler's retreat: He must tell customers what they want to know *insofar as* they have a right to know and ought to know. The "insofar as" is editorial insertion, but it is implicit. And the jeweler, of course, will be the judge of "right" and "ought." So number 4 also winds up saying nothing.

Number 10 comes closest to saying something concrete. But a little reflection upon each of the condemned practices reveals the existence of an escape hatch. When is a trade-in allowance deceitful? How is a fictitious list price distinguished from a price set with fingers crossed? Comparative prices in jewelry retailing are so varied and confusing that almost anything can truthfully be said about them. When does a sale to increase consumer contacts become bait advertising? What makes a sale "fake"—especially in a trade where individual discounts are so common? How, finally, does the jeweler distinguish between "practices which prey upon human ignorance and gullibility" and acceptable techniques of salesmanship? If the jeweler is a man disposed to take his ethical obligations seriously, he may find comfort in reading *The Tradesman's Calling* by the seventeenth-century Puritan clergyman Richard Steele, who asserted that "the sincere Christian . . . must not, indeed, deceive or oppress his neighbor, but need not fly to the other extreme, be righteous overmuch, or refuse to 'take the advantage which the Providence of God puts into his hands.' " [4]

The likely outcome is that the jeweler will make his decision not upon the basis of the code which he has accepted, but in a manner calculated to secure the highest possible long-term profit for his business—consistent with his own subjective and even somewhat amorphous ethical standards. Literally and rigorously adhered to, the code would quickly bankrupt a jeweler. Profit maximization is a more intelligible decision rule, and one with which a businessman can live. The code will be framed and posted prominently on the wall where it can be of maximum effectiveness—in public relations.

ALL THAT GLITTERS

The "Statement of Principles" of the National Electrical Manufacturers Association reveals some additional aspects of industry ethical codes. [5] In February of 1961, Judge J. Cullen Ganey had sent seven of the industry's executives to jail, put twenty-three others on probation, and assessed nearly two million dollars in fines as a climax to the electrical conspiracy case. Huge treble-damage suits under the Sherman Act still loomed ahead of the conspiring firms. In June of 1961 the association adopted its "Statement of Principles." Not surprisingly, it turned out to be a ringing defense of free and open competition and a solemn condemnation of conspiratorial pricing. To assert that the motive was public relations is not to deny that many in the industry had genuinely repented. Industry codes of ethics will probably always be written with an eye more to public relations than the actual conduct of business.

An additional clue to the function that ethical codes may have is provided by the subtle suggestion in many such codes that unethical practices result from too much competition. "Unfair" pricing and miscellaneous "unfair" competitive practices are mentioned repeatedly by businessmen as the most serious ethical problems in their industry.[6] There can be little doubt that many businessmen would welcome an ethical code with real teeth if there were any possibility that such a code could reduce the pressures of competition. "Fair" and "ethical" too often mean noncompetitive. Witness the so-called fair trade laws ardently supported by small businessmen and the numerous "ethical practices" acts through which state legislatures, at the urging of industry lobbies, have attempted to outlaw price and other forms of competition. A "chiseler" is another businessman offering to sell at a price below your own. He will be tagged as a monopolist, a predator, a speculator, a sweater of labor, an outside troublemaker, and, if all else fails, as "un-American." In any event, certainly unethical. Many industry codes hint broadly that competition is the real ethical problem to be corrected. The industry interest in such codes is obvious. The public interest is a different matter altogether.

THE FATAL FLAW

Of the making of codes there is no end. But with the best of intentions they will all run aground on the twin reefs of excessive generality and excessive detail. The problem is not so much rooted in the structure of business or the peculiar complexities of the economic system as in the nature of ethical rules themselves. They cannot be made to perform the task that we are here assigning them because ethical rules neither resolve ethical dilemmas nor create ethical men. There *are* genuine ethical dilemmas which businessmen face, and there *are* unethical people in the business community. But ethical rules make no contribution to the resolution of either problem. It is important to keep in mind the distinction between ethics and law. Law is designed to control behavior, to discourage certain forms of activity and encourage others. Its sanctions are the familiar carrot and stick. But when we speak of an ethical code, we mean a set of rules which do not have these sanctions, which men will obey because they have recognized their appropriateness and given their free consent. The moment coercive sanctions are introduced we stop speaking of ethical rules and begin to speak of legal commands. No one will deny that commands can resolve dilemmas.

But neither commands nor ethical rules will create ethical men. On this, religion, philosophy, and common sense all agree. A thoroughly unscrupulous businessman will not be persuaded to mend his ways by an ethical code any more than thieves will be reformed by a reading of the criminal statutes.

It follows, then, that the most we can hope for from ethical codes is the resolution of ethical dilemmas. But this turns out to be a vain hope. For ethical rules are merely *verbal* resolutions of dilemmas. Each time they are put to work they prove finally deficient, either because they are too vague or because they fail to persuade.

We can most easily clarify this point by examining some of the ethical dilemmas that businessmen encounter. We shall use the ones posed by Raymond Baumhart in introducing his study of the ethics of contemporary businessmen.

> What would you do if, as a director of a large corporation,
> you learned at a board meeting of an impending merger with
> a smaller company? Suppose this company has had an un-
> profitable year, and its stock is selling at a price so low that
> you are certain it will rise when news of the merger becomes
> public knowledge. Would you buy some stock? Or tell a
> friend? Or tell your broker? [7]

Here is a real dilemma, one which has undoubtedly trou-
bled many businessmen at times. Can we formulate an ethical
rule which will resolve this kind of dilemma?

It is widely agreed that *some* ways of enhancing one's
wealth are unfair because they "take advantage" of others.
At the same time it must be admitted that a wide variety of
legitimate ways to increase one's wealth also, in some sense,
"take advantage." Someone who hears a news bulletin on the
radio and immediately phones his broker "takes advantage"
of those who do not happen to be listening to the radio. To
get there first is always to take advantage of those who, for
whatever reason, cannot arrive until later. But not every instance of this sort is "unfair."

We may therefore lay down the ethical rule for stock
trading: Do not take unfair advantage of others. This is a
general rule and one which will command universal assent.
But that is because it says nothing except "Be ethical." And
we hardly resolve an ethical dilemma merely by telling people
to behave ethically. To help in the resolution of such dilemmas we must become more specific. Yet the moment we do so,
we start to lose universal assent; and the more specific we become, the more debatable become the rules we enunciate.

We can try the rule: Do not take unfair advantage of
others *by employing inside information*. This sounds work-
able, but only upon first inspection. What is "inside information"? Just how public does information have to be before it
ceases to be "inside information"? In the last analysis, every

successful stock purchase is based either on pure luck or on inside information—"inside" in the sense that the information or its meaning is not known to everyone in the market for stocks. An investor who consistently refused to employ any inside information would be reduced to buying stocks at random.

This isn't even the end of the matter. One of the social functions performed by rising stock prices is to make easier the accumulation of additional capital by the firms whose stock is going up. The rise represents a judgment by society that optimal resource use calls for the allocation of additional capital to that firm. Thus the informed and intelligent assessment of a corporation's prospects is a social device for securing the best use of resources. A wholesale condemnation of trading on the basis of inside information would amount to a rejection of the stock market as a rational technique for resource allocation. What could be put in its place?

If we wish to formulate an ethical rule which will draw a precise line between advantage and unfair advantage, we shall be compelled to write a book. Every situation has some elements not present in any other situation, and reasonable men will disagree case by case on their significance. Present SEC rules on stock trading by corporate insiders are an example. Many say they go too far and impose unfair burdens on corporate officers and employees. But others claim they leave too many loopholes. Both sides are probably correct. It is impossible to formulate a rule that everyone will accept as fair, without remaining so vague that the rule provides no concrete directives.

This is in no sense to be construed as a condemnation of present SEC regulations. But these are laws, not ethical rules. They condemn broad categories of behavior, as law inevitably must, and leave it to the courts and individual consciences to determine their application. They cannot be made so specific as to require no further interpretation.

CONSCIENCE AND RULES

But is that not precisely what is being argued for by those
who wish to supplement the law with ethical codes? Since
the law cannot cover all possibilities, we need ethical codes
in addition to law. Even the courts cannot provide the degree
of specificity required; as the paragraph above admitted, conscience must also be called in. And ethical rules are intended
to serve as a guide for conscience.

But our point is that they cannot do so. To say that we
must finally rely upon conscience is to say that explicit rules
cannot resolve genuine dilemmas, that we must finally leave
to the judgment of individuals what these rules mean and
how they ought to be applied. Conscience judges ethical
rules, not the other way around. If 95 percent of the people
in an industry agreed that a particular act was unethical, the
other 5 percent could still "in good conscience" commit that
act. Consciences just are not bound—we all know this from
our own experience—by the ethical rules which others lay
down unless these rules command individual, inner assent.
But if they do, there is no point in laying down the rules!

Perhaps the categories of theology can help us here. In
Judaeo-Christian theology, ethical codes are actually called
"law." Hence they are subject to the limitations of law in that
they can always be circumvented by rationalization. The legal-
ist is not an ethical man; he is merely a man of the law, of the
letter but not of the spirit. Therefore the law does not finally
create good behavior any more than it creates good men. It
can lay down broad limits and enforce their observance
through appropriate sanctions. But law is itself incapable of
securing what it ultimately desires: that men "do justice, love
mercy, and walk humbly." Legalism can be effective to some
degree in controlling behavior through punishments and rewards, meted out in predictable fashion for acts that can be

precisely defined. But it has limitations, the limitations of all
literalism, and ethical codes can in no way overcome these
limitations.

Let us try another example, the second ethical dilemma
used by Raymond Baumhart to introduce his study.

> What would you do if as president of a company in a highly
> competitive industry, you learned that a competitor had made
> an important scientific discovery which would give him a
> substantial advantage over you? If you had an opportunity
> to hire one of his employees who knew the details of the dis-
> covery, would you do it? [8]

Why not? There are some very good reasons why he
should not be hired, but none of them has much to do with
ethics. The discovery may be protected by patent, so that his
knowledge will be of no use. Or the details known to him may
not be sufficient to enable you to duplicate your competitor's
innovation. Perhaps you will be unwilling to set a precedent
with dangerous implications, especially if your own firm is
vulnerable to such employee raids. Then there is the threat of
legal action to be considered. The courts have sometimes held
that an employee may not disclose privileged information
upon taking a position with another employer and that an
employer "betrayed" in this fashion may sue for damages. Or
perhaps the prospective employee demands more in compen-
sation than he is likely to be worth. If none of these considerations seems relevant, why not hire him?

"It just wouldn't be ethical." This is the response many
businessmen would give. But why not? The fact that the discovery has not been patented suggests that the discovering
firm has no clear and unassailable right to exclusive enjoy-
ment of its benefits. The fact that there is little danger of
court action suggests the same thing. It is admittedly unethical to "steal" another firm's property, including its trade
secrets, but what constitutes stealing? Stealing presupposes a

property right; but just what are the property rights in this case?

If no clear property rights can be discerned and a firm nonetheless declines to hire such an employee, it is just as likely that the firm is refusing to compete vigorously as that it is behaving ethically. Owners of professional football teams who refuse to bid for the services of those who have played out their options with another club are clearly trying to avoid the consequences of competition. They know that free and competitive bidding will result in a reallocation of some of the profits from owners to players, and they don't want that for obvious reasons. They are behaving sensibly; but it requires a perversion of logic to claim that they are also behaving ethically.

No one can lay down in advance the precise circumstances under which it is or is not ethical to hire a competitor's employees. This does not mean ethics will not enter a decision. It does mean that no ethical code will resolve such dilemmas.

GENERAL RULES VERSUS SPECIFIC CIRCUMSTANCES

Baumhart provides three more brief examples at which we shall glance:

What do you think about—

. . . an executive earning $10,000 a year who has been padding his expense account by about $500 a year?

. . . an executive owning stock in a company with which his own company regularly does business?

. . . the idea that management should act in the interest of shareholders alone? [9]

Let us take them one by one. No one approves of "padding," but this is because padding *means* claiming unjustified reimbursement. The real question is what constitutes padding? How shall we draw the line between necessary and frivolous expenditures? On what grounds are we to condemn an executive who lives frugally on the road so that he can bring home a little extra to reward his family for his absences? Some firms regard the expense account as a fringe benefit, though others do not; this will make a difference. There just are no ethical rules that can adequately define padding. Clarity in the tax laws and in a company's policy toward expense accounts can make a major contribution toward resolving these dilemmas, and it is probably here that the problem should be tackled. Businessmen will still have to be guided by their consciences to some extent; but it is their consciences plus tax law and company policies that will guide them, and not a set of ethical rules.

An executive who owns stock in a supplying company is more foolish than unethical. The interesting thing is that such a man may bend over backwards to be fair and thus be *un*-fair to the supplier in whom he has an interest. Some conflicts of this sort may be practically unavoidable; a large corporation could do business with so many other corporations that any executive with a diversified portfolio of stocks would find himself compromised. Common sense, and not ethics, dictates that an executive should refuse to hold any stocks which might embarrass him were his ownership made public. Ethical rules can contribute nothing beyond that, although conscience will inevitably play a role.

As for the third question, in whose interest *should* management act if not in the interests of shareholders? It is easy enough to run down the familiar list of suppliers, consumers, employees, and the general public, but to none of them does management have a definable responsibility. In principle, management is answerable to the owners of the enterprise, and all its acts must be judged by the contribution they make to the continued viability and profitability of the enterprise. The loud proclamation of additional responsibilities may be good public relations, or it may contribute to management's sense of benevolence, but it is not in itself ethical. And no ethical code is capable of telling a corporate manager when he may or should sacrifice the shareholders' interest to some competing claim.

THE OTHER SIDE OF THE COIN

Ethical rules can even make ethical behavior *less* likely. A rule can be used as an excuse for not deciding, for avoiding the burden of choice. The fact that we can sometimes hide behind ethical rules may be another explanation for their popularity. But a genuinely ethical man will refuse to surrender his responsibilities to an abstract and possibly irrelevant set of rules.

Ethics is important in the conduct of business, as it is in the conduct of all of life. But we do not advance the cause of ethics by pretending that ethical behavior can be created through the enunciation of ethical rules. This kind of legalism is more likely to subvert than it is to promote the quality of conduct toward which it is ostensibly directed.

Whatever businessmen may say about ethics, they almost always behave as if good ethics were simply good business.[10] They may deny that profit maximization is the criterion of social responsibility, but they will nonetheless act in the manner best calculated to maximize profits. With these assertions we are not so much indicting businessmen for hypocrisy as crediting them with the sense to recognize where empty cant must end and responsible decisions begin.

No one has yet succeeded in defining the social responsibilities of businessmen in any useful way. The vague pronouncements to be found in industry manifestos or corporate policy statements or at the end of university seminars wind up saying only "Be responsible and ethical," and leave it to the businessman to decide what that will mean in practice. When the time of decision arrives, however, the businessman decides in just the same way that he would have decided had he not been informed about his social responsibilities. Law provides the framework; mores, habits, conventions, prudential rules, and whatever values he entertains provide the matrix; and the criterion is maximum anticipated profit.

No one will deny this more loudly than businessmen, which is only to be expected in view of the connotations the public unfortunately attaches to profit maximization. What is really surprising is that a large and growing number outside the business community also insist that the typical American businessman has abandoned profit maximization in favor of a broader conception of his social responsibilities. We have already argued that this would not necessarily be to his credit. We also maintain, as a matter of simple realism, that it is not true.

FORMS OF SELF-DECEPTION

Suppose that a businessman has accepted the responsibility to do his part in protecting America's balance-of-payments position, in accord with the admonitions of the President and the Secretary of the Treasury. This means that he will now scrutinize carefully all overseas investment projects and cut back on those projects which are not in the national interest. What real impact will this policy have? What new criteria will he now employ? A wholesale reduction of foreign investment will improve the short-term balance-of-payments position, but at the expense of the long-term position. If the businessman therefore decides to undertake only those projects which will in the long run make the maximum contribution to strength in America's balance-of-payments position, he implicitly makes use of the maximum-profit criterion. The real change effected will be in his rhetoric.

Numerous businessmen have accepted a responsibility to control the advances of "automation" in the public interest. This clearly does not mean that they have committed themselves to a static technology. It means that they will introduce technological innovations "carefully." But what does "carefully" mean? If a business firm is convinced that a particular bit of "automating" will substantially reduce costs, this becomes responsible automation. If a project, on the other hand, holds out slight promises and will moreover precipitate serious difficulties with the union, this is irresponsible automation. This *is* roughly the way businessmen look at the issue; and when the clouds of rhetoric have dispersed they are seen to be deciding upon the basis of maximum anticipated profit to the enterprise.

If a long-time employee is no longer capable of doing his job, should he be demoted or dismissed? The businessman who proclaims his ethical responsibilities toward such employees is well aware of the potentialy disastrous effects on employee morale of a ruthless personnel policy. Successful profit maximization requires attention to far more—and more subtle—variables than just physical productivity and explicit costs. Many employers will keep such a man on, perhaps at a slight reduction in pay or privileges, and will even believe that in doing so they have set social responsibility above maximum profit. But we all like to believe that our motives are purer than they actually are.

The human capacity for rationalization is infinite. How many times have we known anyone to commit an act which he himself regarded as unethical? There are always special circumstances to be adduced, vague probabilities to be assessed, competing claims that can be appealed to. The businessman caught up in the concrete tasks of decision making knows that his power to decide effectively is narrowly confined by economic constraints—the constraints of anticipated costs and revenue. He instinctively and rightly rejects any suggestions which fail to recognize these limitations and give them their appropriate weight. When all the talk about social responsibility has ended, the businessman knows that he faces a rather limited range of viable alternatives and that he may not choose arbitrarily among them. Profit is the test of his success, the foundation of his enterprise's existence, the source of that power without which he would have *no* freedom to choose. When the chips are down, therefore, he looks to profitability as the criterion for his actions, and his social responsibilities are redefined to match his decisions.

This is not a habit in any way peculiar to businessmen. From the ridiculous through the sublime, the golfer justifies his time spent on the links, the student justifies his failure to prepare, the rake justifies his philandering, the South African justifies *apartheid*, the Marxist justifies revolution, and the businessman justifies his pursuit of maximum profits. Explicit ethical rules in such a context will be viewed as something to be interpreted, not slavishly obeyed. And such a view is finally right. For the ethical man cannot be defined in terms of rules. Ultimately, it is the ethical man who decides what is right.

Notes to Chapter V.

[1] Norman C. Miller, *The Great Salad Oil Swindle* (Coward-McCann, Inc., New York, 1965).

[2] Joseph C. Towle, editor of the papers and addresses in *Ethics and Standards in American Business* (Houghton Mifflin Company, Boston, 1964), states that "the increased awareness of ethical problems in business indicates that more explicit professional and ethical standards for administrative behavior will be required in the future" (p. 19). He offers this as a fair summary of the position taken by the various contributors to the volume. Appendixes to the book put on display varied codes of ethics, presumably as models.

[3] The code is included in appendix B of Towle's very useful collection (*op. cit.*, pp. 281–282).

[4] Quoted in Richard Tawney, *Religion and the Rise of Capitalism* (Harcourt, Brace, & World, Inc., New York, 1926; Mentor Books, New American Library of World Literature, Inc., 1947), p. 204 (in Mentor edition).

[5] It may also be found in Towle, *op. cit.*, pp. 277–279.

[6] Raymond C. Baumhart asked businessmen to list the unethical practices they would most like to see eliminated from their industries. "Gifts, gratuities, bribes, and 'call girls'" ranked first in his tabulation. But even a casual inspection of his categories reveals that the most detested unethical practice is pushing for additional sales. The word "unfair" is used very loosely to cover a multitude of complaints which probably boil down to this. Baumhart, "How Ethical Are Businessmen?" *Harvard Business Review* (July–August, 1961), especially p. 160. We are all disposed to cry "foul" when we lose a point.

[7] *Ibid.*, p. 7.

[8] *Ibid.*

[9] *Ibid.*

[10] They admit this implicitly when they argue, as so many do, that the unethical businessman will lose out in the long run. A shift in emphasis yields the argument that what is most compatible with long-run business profitability and success must be ethical.

VI.

Another Look at Competition

A crucial question can be postponed no longer. If new conceptions of social responsibility and new definitions of business ethics cannot be relied upon to constrain the businessman in his exercise of social power, how will his power be constrained?

The classical answer, of course, is the market within the framework of law. But this answer no longer commands general assent. The power of the businessman has supposedly grown so great that the market can no longer restrain it within socially acceptable bounds. And law is too cumbersome, too dangerous even, to close the gap satisfactorily. We appear to come back continually to the concept of social responsibility, not because it has proved its worth but because all the alternatives are unacceptable.

Does the market control the American businessman today? Or do businessmen control the market? Until we have achieved some measure of agreement on how competitive the American economy is today, we can have little hope of reaching agreement on how the power of the businessman ought to be controlled in the public interest.

WHERE IS THE EVIDENCE?

The reason that opinions differ so widely on this question is that we have achieved no concensus on the kind of evidence which is relevant to an answer.

Data on absolute size, though often cited as evidence, indicate little if anything. The fact that General Motors had sales of 17 billion dollars in 1964 proves that General Motors is indeed large but not that it possesses significant monopoly power.

The percentage of total industrial assets or total employment or total sales enjoyed by the largest 100 or 200 industrial firms also means little. Aggregate data of this type are impressive, but they say almost nothing about market power.

Industrial concentration ratios have often been treated as useful indices of the degree of competition or monopoly in an industry. If the percentage of total sales going to the four largest firms in a particular industry exceeds 70 or 50 or 30 percent, that industry is adjudged not highly competitive. But such data are difficult to interpret. The number of firms in the industry may be more important than the concentration ratio.

There is also the problem of defining an industry. Given a sufficiently narrow definition, every industry could be made to show a high concentration ratio. To define an industry relevantly, attention must be directed to the degree to which products compete with one another. But this raises a host of problems. A manufacturer on the East Coast may be in only marginal competition with a manufacturer on the West Coast, despite the similarity of their products. Two products that are physically unrelated may compete fiercely for certain uses, such as steel and concrete, or glass and tin.

Industrial concentration ratios can be calculated easily enough, but deciding upon their meaning is another matter. It is interesting, moreover, that they lend very little real support to the notion that competition has declined in the American economy. One definitive study of concentration in manufacturing from 1901 to 1947 concludes with this summary statement: "The odds are better than even that there has actually been *some* decline in concentration. It is a good bet that there has at least been no actual increase; and the odds do seem high against any substantial increase." [1] The widely held notion that competition must have declined since the beginning of this century because industries have become so much more concentrated simply does not square with the available evidence. [2]

What about the well-known phenomenon of administered prices? The fact that most prices no longer fluctuate in response to supply or demand changes seems to prove that firms have the power to set and rigidly administer prices. This would not be possible if the economy were genuinely competitive.

But this argument, popular though it is, turns out to be demonstration by assumption. And the assumption is extremely dubious. A leading student of the monopoly problem, after commenting on economists' largely fruitless search for an explanation of rigid prices, adds this telling comment: "It appears that the real world has been equally remiss in supplying the phenomena they were seeking to explain." [3] Even list or catalog prices are generally not as rigid as is popularly assumed. And in any event, the price actually charged is what counts, with appropriate allowances for all such quality changes as delivery times and reliability, special services, and other extras.

Sometimes the plight of the small businessman is cited as evidence. It used to be possible, supposedly, for anyone with a little capital and a lot of determination to establish himself in an industry. But today the big firms have things all their own way. You have to be huge to succeed. This line of argument is so vague and begs so many questions that it is almost impossible to refute—undoubtedly one of its advantages. Was there ever such a golden era for small business? Are the big firms efficient because they are big or big because they have been efficient in the past? Is it true that small business is increasingly at a disadvantage? And in any event, the failure of competitors is by no means the same thing as the decline of competition. Vigorous competition will always affect the less efficient adversely, and a high rate of business failure may prove that an industry is competitive rather than that only monopolists can succeed in it.

WHAT DO WE MEAN BY COMPETITION?

As it turns out, not only have we achieved no consensus on how competition should be measured; substantial disagreement exists even on what is meant by competition. But if we intend to derive policy conclusions from our assessment of the extent to which competition or monopoly is dominant in the American economy, our definition of competition must be relevant to the problem.

In economic theory, *pure competition* is one pole of the competition-monopoly spectrum. In an industry characterized by pure competition, there are no legal restrictions on entry into the industry, no single firm has the power to alter the price of the product through its own action, and there is no collusion among firms.

Each firm will consequently be a "price-taker": It will sell at the price determined in the market. Any attempt to charge a higher price will be frustrated because buyers will be able to obtain all they want from competing firms at the going market price. Under pure competition, then, no firm has the power to set prices, and in the absence of collusion what cannot be done individually is also not done concertedly.

Moreover, with no legal restrictions on entry, price will tend continually toward cost of production. This is because any price substantially higher, by yielding a positive net revenue, will lead to the creation of new capacity. Existing firms will attempt to expand in order to enlarge their profits, and new firms will be attracted. The ensuing increase in supply will push the price down toward cost of production.

Pure competition is an abstraction, of course. But it provides a theoretical norm useful in determining the degree of competition faced by any firm. Power over price and the level of profits are the two criteria suggested by this norm. If we can demonstrate that a particular firm lacks significant power over price and that the price it receives tends continually toward cost of production, we shall have established that the firm is competitive. While this is a matter of definition, the definition we are using has the merit of focusing attention on what are commonly regarded as the vices of monopoly: The monopolist has the power to raise and maintain the price significantly above cost of production and thereby earn an "inequitable" profit.

Let us state our conclusion first. The American economy is far more workably competitive today than we commonly assume, and the tendency within this century has been decidedly in the direction of more competition rather than less. Can this conclusion be supported?

SOME NEGLECTED ASPECTS

Since it is easier to argue for the second than the first half of our conclusion, let us begin there. What reasons do we have for supposing that the tendency has been strongly in the direction of more vigorous competition? There are principally three: transportation, technology, and information.

Geography is an important source of monopoly power. There can be hundreds of producers of a given item and still very little competition if none of the producers is able to market his product in the vicinity of another. The significance of transportation is immediately apparent. A number of examples may help the reader to see just how important a role transportation does play in breaking down or reducing monopoly power.

The retail grocery industry has been revolutionized within the last quarter century. Large "supermarkets," offering a wide range of products at notoriously modest markups, are the rule where only a generation ago they were the exception. The principle which has created them is that a respectable profit can be earned through large volume and small markup as well as through large markups with small volume. But it was the family automobile which made the supermarkets possible, by enlarging the potential market area of each grocery store. Moreover, the fact that the housewife-on-wheels can readily choose among a number of stores some distance from her home compels grocery stores to be competitive. The resulting struggle to pare costs, improve service, and keep prices attractive is just what we mean by competition, and the consumer has been the beneficiary.

The most important source of monopoly power in the early nineteenth century may well have been the advantage conferred by geographic isolation. The railroad began to change all that in the 1840s. Low shipping costs brought scattered producers into competition with one another. The consumer received a wider range of choice, and producers began to face intensified competitive pressure. What the railroads began, trucks completed. The combination of the internal combustion engine and an excellent highway system has extended the advantages of competition to consumers in the most scattered byways of the country.

MARKET INTERPENETRATION

Technological advances have played a similar role. We are not using the term in the narrow sense of improvements in the production process, but in the very broad sense of improvements in "technique." Progress in machinery design, quality control, product development, and marketing methods are all embraced by the phrase "technological advances." Their effect has been decidedly in the direction of extending market interpenetration. Once again examples will serve to make the point most easily.

The demand for steel is often described as highly inelastic. Sizable increases in the price of steel will not result in a large fall in sales volume because there are, supposedly, no substitutes for steel. This situation gives substantial pricing power to firms in the steel industry. This power may still be excessive, particularly in view of certain pricing habits in the steel industry, but it has been declining because of technological advances. There *are* substitutes for steel; not in all uses, of course, but in a large and growing number of uses. Concrete, aluminum, plastic, and plywood as well as thinner gauges are all substitutes for steel under the right circumstances. A high price for steel provides an incentive for users to seek new ways of economizing on steel, and their search has often proved dramatically effective. As the technological knowledge of potential steel users has expanded, the elasticity of demand for steel has increased. And this amounts to a reduction in whatever amount of monopoly power firms in the steel industry possess.

When the Xerox Corporation first put its revolutionary copying machine on the market, the reception was enthusiastic. The immediate reward was a generous profit for those who had developed the process. But even the patent privilege did not protect these profits from erosion. Other firms, eager to capitalize on the unexpectedly large demand for this kind of equipment, struggled successfully to develop products that could compete with the Xerox copier. Within only a few years, the technological ingenuity of other manufacturers had created a highly competitive industry, offering to consumers a wide range of copying machines and compelling Xerox to improve its product and reduce its prices.[4]

We have already referred to the practical difficulties of defining an industry. These difficulties have in large part been created by the technological ingenuity of American businesses as they struggle to enlarge their potential markets by developing new products that cut across established product lines. The consequence of this process for society is, once again, ongoing market interpenetration and its corollary, continual erosion of positions of monopoly power.

Most such developments are quite unspectacular, likely to be overlooked or just taken for granted. But it would be difficult to exaggerate the role which they play in invigorating competition in the production and marketing of goods and services.

THE KNOWLEDGEABLE CONSUMER

A powerful impediment to vigorous competition is ignorance. If potential buyers do not know what they are looking for in a product, or how well different products meet their specifications, or what alternative products are available and on what terms, they will choose less effectively among suppliers' offers. But as more consumers acquire this kind of information, the pressure on suppliers to improve their offers intensifies. Even if only a small percentage of potential customers are astute shoppers, the struggle of competitors to get or retain their trade will extend the advantages of competition to less sophisticated buyers. The housewife who never pays attention to prices and always shops at the same stores might reflect some time on how much she owes to those relatively few who do shop around and who are always trying to ferret out bargains.

Much has been written about the ignorance and gullibility of the American consumer. Some of it is well taken, but most of it is highly exaggerated. More education plus the "information explosion" have almost certainly increased the typical consumer's ability to get his money's worth. While only a few read consumers' magazines, these few can and do function as a cutting edge, providing a measure of additional protection to the less knowledgeable or acute. The discernible drift in advertising away from the endless repetition of meaningless slogans toward the communication of information is indirect evidence of the consumer's increasing sophistication. The years ahead will probably witness a continuation and acceleration of this change.

The result is the steady erosion of monopoly power based on ignorance and the emergence of another factor making for increased competition in the American economy.

THE EXTENT OF COMPETITION

The evidence points time and again to the same conclusion: The American economy is becoming more rather than less competitive, and the forces which work continually to erode positions of monopoly power far outweigh those which operate in the other direction. But the basic question for many is not the direction in which we are moving but where we are currently. Is competition today an adequate regulator of the economy?

This question is more difficult to answer because it presupposes agreement on how much competition would be adequate. Yet a surprising number of those who condemn the contemporary performance of the American economy on the grounds that monopoly rather than competition is its dominant feature concede that at one time the economy was genuinely competitive. If so, and if competition has increased, it is surely competitive now. Of course, it is slippery business to hoist someone on his own petard. We cannot reject an argument on the grounds of irrelevant evidence and faulty logic but then employ it to plug a hole in our own case. We have contended that those who seek to assess the degree to which the American economy is currently competitive have too often been unclear both on their definition of competition and on the kind of evidence required to make their case.

But strong evidence of another sort is certainly available. The past performance of the American economy gives little reason to suppose that it has been hobbled by inadequate competition. By almost any criteria that can be suggested, the United States has been an economic success. A marked trend in the direction of more vigorous and more effective competition certainly lends strong support, therefore, to the conclusion that the American economy is adequately competitive today.

The most important implication of such a conclusion is that the problem of business power has been grossly exaggerated. We have been groping anxiously for a definition of the businessman's social responsibilities because we have failed to see how narrowly the businessman is in fact restrained by the market. We have too readily accepted the myth, perpetrated by some businessmen as well as business critics, that our fate is in the hands of a small number of business executives. This is simply not true.

The economic resources of this nation are today allocated overwhelmingly in accord with the dictates of the market. It is society which commands the businessman, and not the other way around. Businessmen can and do decide contrary to the market—sometimes consciously, more often on the basis of faulty information and forecasts. But the penalty for the businessman who prefers his personal notion of social welfare to the wishes of society as expressed through the market is a reduction in power. And in this way society—not the conscience of the businessman—compels responsibility in the exercise of private power.

A SPECULATIVE POSTSCRIPT

The thoughtful reader will be disturbed at this point. If competition and not monopoly is the dominant fact in the American economy today, why have so many intelligent and informed people assumed just the opposite? Though we can only speculate, the question merits an answer.

One explanation could be the "General Motors complex." A surprisingly large number of people seem to assume that General Motors is the most typical American business firm. The undeniable fact that it is extremely untypical does not keep people from documenting the most sweeping generalizations by citing the power or the size of General Motors (or sometimes United States Steel). Even General Motors does not have the degree of market power that many people uncritically impute to the "average" firm. More importantly, there are other firms besides General Motors and other industries in addition to the automobile industry.

Another and related explanation would be the usual human tendency to notice only the spectacular. Small firms and highly competitive firms do not make the newspapers as often as the largest firms and the firms which may be able to exercise a substantial amount of monopoly power. The need here is for perspective, for closer attention to the whole picture rather than selected and perhaps unsavory aspects. Related to this is the fact that we take good economic performance for granted and only think about competition and monopoly when we come to suspect that we are being inadequately served.

But the most important part of any explanation is probably the low level of economic sophistication that characterizes so much of the literature in this field. Market power is an economic concept, and it is not likely to be discussed intelligently by a writer unfamiliar with the basic notions of economic analysis. The bulk of the pronouncements which appear on this topic and which create public thinking on the issue are not written by economists, much less by economists who have specialized in the area of monopoly and public policy.

Finally, the "fact" of monopoly is a convenient justification for all sorts of policy proposals that actually originate elsewhere. We are all reluctant to abandon a useful premise for any reason so insubstantial as that it contradicts the available evidence. The "dominant position of monopolists and oligopolists" in our economy will enjoy the comfortable status of an a priori fact as long as so many groups find it a powerful argument in support of their own special pleading.

Notes to Chapter VI.

[1] M. I. Adelman, "The Measurement of Industrial Concentration," *Review of Economics and Statistics* (November, 1951), pp. 292–293.

[2] A useful summary of the evidence may be found in Clair Wilcox, *Public Policies toward Business,* 3d ed. (Richard D. Irwin, Inc., Homewood, Ill., 1966), pp. 275–279.

[3] George J. Stigler, "Administered Prices and Oligopolistic Inflation," *Journal of Business* (January, 1962), p. 8.

[4] The current competitiveness of the industry can be inferred from the advertisements for copying machines that take up so much space today in business publications.

VII.

Power: Its Nature and Control

T he preceding chapter attempted to show that we have been much too eager to dismiss competition as a regulating force in the American economy. The power of the businessman in our society has been seriously exaggerated because we have mistakenly assumed effective competition to be a thing of the past. But competition is still the rule, not the exception.

Nonetheless, there are those exceptions. Monopoly power does exist, and where it exists we have no assurances of a satisfactory business performance. Shall we rely in these situations upon the businessman's sense of his social responsibilities? Or are there better alternatives?

In the American tradition, power which is open to abuse must be restrained by power—not by conscience. The belief that no person or group is to be trusted with the power to act irresponsibly runs deep in American thought and life. Is there good reason to abandon that tradition here? Or have we failed to see that this is what we are doing when we call upon the conscience of the businessman to control the power which he possesses?

There are some who will argue that the businessman does not actually possess power and that the entire question is for that reason inappropriate. Since we have for the most part been jousting with those who exaggerate the businessman's power, it may be high time to tackle those who would define it away. But in the process we shall see that power is not a simple phenomenon, that analogies drawn from the political world are not completely applicable to the economic realm, and that some of our most popular notions about the way to control monopoly power rest upon a dubious argument by analogy.

THE NATURE OF POWER

Power is the crucial concept in any system of social ethics or political thought, and the use and control of power have been a focus of human interest since the beginning of history. Mankind's continuing concern with the problem of justice has been at root a concern with the distribution of power. Men have always held, though with different emphases and applications, that each person is in justice entitled to possess and use an appropriate amount of power. To how much power is each entitled? What restrictions should be placed upon its exercise? In what ways can power be enhanced?

The last question is usually treated as a different problem altogether because of our unfortunate habit of supposing that power is in itself dangerous or unjust. Many writers, for example, regard freedom as a good and consider power the arch enemy of freedom. The result has been a widespread but thoroughly untenable belief that anything which reduces power extends freedom. What makes this notion so misleading is the fact that freedom *is* power and power *is* freedom.

No person could have freedom if he lacked power. And it would be meaningless to assert that someone possessed power if he lacked all freedom. Freedom in the most general sense is the power to be and to do: to exist, to act, to influence events and alter outcomes. A man who is crippled loses power and hence a measure of his freedom. A man who is imprisoned is said to have lost his freedom precisely because he has lost the power to order and control the conditions of his existence. If the power of a nation is reduced in any way, its freedom of international maneuver is thereby reduced. If the freedom of a businessman is diminished by laws and regulations, his power as a businessman is correspondingly diminished. It makes just as much sense to say that freedom conflicts with freedom and power with power as to say that power and freedom come into conflict. And it may prove a more useful way of putting the matter.

The framers of the American Constitution have been extolled as men exceptionally aware of the dangers posed by political power. This verdict of later generations would have surprised some of their contemporaries. For it was the opponents of ratification and not the proponents who in 1789 spoke ominously of the dangers of a strong central government. Those who favored continuing under the Articles of Confederation rather than adopting the new Constitution were the true enemies of governmental power.

And that was precisely the weakness in their case. A government without power is a contradiction in terms, and a government with inadequate power is an inadequate government. The men who framed the American Constitution were not so much afraid of power as they were sophisticated in their understanding of its nature. They were the best friends of freedom in 1789 because they recognized that freedom could not exist in the absence of power and therefore turned their attention to the real problem: What kind of freedom and what kind of power are desirable?

It is even possible to speak of government freedom once we recognize that a government has assigned functions. An adequate government will possess the freedom to levy taxes, regulate the currency, raise military forces, and perform all other functions assigned to it. While we more typically speak of the *power* to do all these things, it makes equal sense to speak of the *freedom* to do so. A government is weak if it is not free to take those actions which will lead to the realization of its ends. Many of the newer governments of the world are today faced by exactly this dilemma. Government officials must operate under so many threatening constraints—sectionalism, military ambitions, popular impatience, subversive conspiracies, parochial nationalism—that they do not have the freedom of maneuver requisite for successful accomplishment of their mandate to govern. The virtue of a military dictatorship in such countries, whether of the right or the left, is precisely that it frees the state administrators to use the means they deem necessary for the attainment of desired ends.

But government freedom is the potential enemy of individual freedom. And this is true in two ways. In the American tradition, government is the creature of the governed, charged with the accomplishment of designated tasks and possessing no purposes of its own. The only freedom it should have is the freedom to reach its assigned goals. But because government is composed of men, and men have the habit of equating their own ambitions with the public welfare, actual governments strive continually to enlarge the scope of their freedom beyond the established bounds. This divorce between the will of governed and governor creates one kind of threat to individual freedom.

But there is another threat that would arise even if all politicians were statesmen and all statesmen were saints. Life in society requires limitations upon individual freedom, running the gamut from traffic regulations to criminal statutes. If there were no necessity of curtailing individual freedom, there would be no necessity for government. But governments exist because limitations must be imposed and because they must be effectively enforced.

This does not mean, of course, that men were "born free" and have been enslaved by governments. The limitations which men in a democratic society impose upon themselves and ask government to enforce are limitations designed ultimately to enlarge the freedom of each through curtailing the freedom of all. But this means that individuals can at times find their freedom drastically and intolerably infringed by government. What enlarges the freedom of most or nearly all may radically curtail the freedom of a few.

THE POWER OF THE BUSINESSMAN

Let us return to the businessman. Every businessman has power: the power to organize resources for the attainment of particular ends, the freedom to make effective choices among a variety of possible alternatives. But power is not the same as the power to coerce. And business power differs fundamentally from government power in that the former is *not* coercive.

The special power which the businessman possesses in our society derives from the institution of private property. By protecting the private right to use and dispose of property, within certain limitations, a society promotes the efficient utilization of its resources. It follows that if these limitations are too narrowly drawn, society will fail to secure the practical benefits of private property. Another way of putting the matter is to say that there is some minimum below which the power of the businessman should not be reduced.

But is the opposite also true? Are there equal dangers and disadvantages in drawing these limits too broadly? This question cannot be given a simple answer because the limitations which are imposed by law on the right of property are not the only, not even the most important, limitations on the business-man's power.

We are often in the habit of speaking as if, in the absence of legal restrictions, a businessman is free to do as he pleases. Without rent controls, landlords are free to gouge tenants. If no minimum standards are set by law, home builders are free to erect poor-quality houses. In the absence of a minimum-wage law, employers are free to pay starvation wages. Since we recognize the impracticability of regulating everything by law, we believe ourselves to be substantially dependent upon the goodwill and sensitive consciences of businessmen. This is the point at which the demand for social responsibility typically emerges. But the demand is premature; for business-men are not in fact free in that way.

At the risk of belaboring the obvious, let us look again at each instance cited above and note what is in fact the most important restraint operating in each case. The power of the landlord is limited primarily by the terms on which other landlords are offering rental units; the power of the home builder by the price and quality of the houses which his com-petitors construct; the power of the employer by the wage offers of other employers in the area. We would be tempted to add the word "obviously" to all this were it not for the fact that so much is regularly written and said in which the ob-vious is omitted. It is certainly possible for someone to hold that these limitations are insufficient in particular cases. But to treat them as nonexistent is to ignore the dominant fact of economic life in a market society.

THE INHERENT RESTRAINT

In a market economy, the power of a businessman to sell or buy on any terms is limited by the alternatives which others

make available. In order to effect a transaction, the businessman must hold out to suppliers or customers an alternative
at least as attractive as all others which they face. To be
effective he must extend the range of alternatives available to
others. All of which to say that the businessman can maintain
and extend his power only by exercising it in a manner which
is the very opposite of coercive.

The necessary caveats can be entered later. The point to
be made is too fundamental to risk letting it be obscured by
qualifications. Success in buying and selling is the condition
of continued power in the business world. The businessman's
power is consequently dependent upon his ability to persuade
customers and suppliers to accept his terms. This can only be
done by offering them an alternative which they find preferable
to all others, that is to say, by extending the range of alternatives which they confront. To do this is to enlarge the freedom
and power of customers and suppliers. The power of the
businessman therefore grows along with, and not in opposition to, the power of those with whom he deals in the market.
That is why the power of the businessman is fundamentally
noncoercive.

For a strong example, consider that favorite villain, the
loan shark. As everyone "knows," loan sharks prey upon the
poor, the defenseless, and the ignorant, compelling them to
pay exorbitant rates of interest to secure the money which
they need. The world would be a far better place without
the loan shark, as everyone agrees—except his victims. They
patronize him. They borrow money on his terms, not because
he compels them to, but because he is the best alternative
available. They *hunt* for him, which is not exactly what one
expects from people about to be coerced and exploited.

Few will be completely happy about a situation in which
many people have no better alternative than to borrow money
at interest rates of 100 percent or even 1,000 percent per year.
But it is the situation which is at fault and not the loan shark.

He extends the range of alternatives available to the people in his neighborhood; and that is the exact opposite of coercion.

This is not an accidental but an essential feature of business power. Those who possess property have the power to dispose of it in accord with their own preferences. But the terms on which they are able to do so are set by the fact that others have a similar power. The fact that a poor man is compelled to pay 10 percent interest per month is not due to the presence of a rapacious loan shark but to the absence of others willing to offer credit on more favorable terms. Those who patronize him would not be better but worse off were he removed from the scene. And the power that he possesses will decline if he fails to enlarge the freedom and power of his potential patrons.

AN IMPORTANT QUALIFICATION

We have drawn out these somewhat abstract reflections upon power in order to counter the misleading notion that all power is alike and must therefore be controlled in the same way. Those who contend that businessmen have no power are really arguing that they lack the power to coerce. This is an important distinction. But it is not enough to compel the conclusion that business power poses no problems for society. If we take a pragmatic view of property rights, we may say that the power to dispose of property has been allowed to remain in the hands of businessmen in the hope that this power will be used to extend the freedom and power of others. In more familiar language, society has certain expectations: It expects above all a continual improvement in the quantity, quality, and variety of national output, and an equitable distribution of that output.

Monopoly power is an obstacle on the path to this goal; on this proposition popular thought and economic analysis agree. But economic analysis diverges from popular thought in suggesting that monopoly power is best viewed as a deficiency, as the consequence of too little of something rather than too much.

Monopoly power is always a matter of degree. There is no such thing as absolute monopoly power because there are substitutes for anything; and this means no one is completely free to establish the terms on which he will do business. Since monopoly power varies inversely with the availability of ready substitutes, the key to establishing and maintaining a monopoly position is the power to exclude substitutes. If someone maintains that a particular business firm enjoys monopoly power, but cannot show any way in which that firm is able successfully to exclude substitutes, he is almost certainly mistaken in his assessment.

The goal of every businessman is to create for himself a position of substantial monopoly power. This is not as shocking as it sounds. The man who builds a better mousetrap or makes a good 5-cent cigar entertains the hope that no one else will be able to match his feat and that those with mice or a yen to smoke will find his product so superior that they will not seriously consider a substitute. But in a genuinely *free* enterprise system, such hopes are doomed to continual disappointment. Competitors rush in to duplicate his accomplishment, good substitutes appear, and his monopoly power is quickly eroded.

But this does not always happen. There are ways to exclude competitors, to keep substitutes out of the market, and thus to build and maintain a position of significant monopoly power. Just being there first, with all the advantages of a large and functioning enterprise, may be enough to discourage potential competitors. But the most effective tactic—and the one on which businessmen most frequently rely—is to invoke the power of the government.

THE CARE AND NURTURE OF MONOPOLY

It is extremely difficult to preserve a position of substantial monopoly power without an assist from government. There are so many present and potential competitors for almost any product in almost any market that the possibility of profit quickly creates competition. If the profit is not only possible but highly probable, as would be the case if an existing firm enjoyed significant monopoly power, the monopolist's market will prove irresistibly attractive to a variety of competitors. They can seldom be excluded effectively unless government is persuaded to lend an assisting hand.

The preservation of privileged market positions is not free enterprise, of course, but it is doubtful that many American businessmen genuinely want free enterprise. They want to be free themselves, free from any kind of interference by government or competitors, and to that end they are often eager to curtail freedom of enterprise for others. The glaring inconsistency between their preaching and their practice is papered over by dubious reasoning and spurious appeals to a larger public good.

Licensing is the paradigm case. Hundreds of businesses and occupations in the United States today can be entered only by those who have a license. Licensing is customarily defended as a means of protecting consumers against incompetence and fraud, but the origins and actual practice of licensing in one industry after another suggest that this defense is the rankest sort of sophistry. The demand for regulation and licensing comes typically from the industry to be regulated! Trucking firms, physicians, television repairmen, pharmacists, interstate movers, dentists, security brokers, morticians, package liquor stores, taxicab operators, and many more have all defended licensing as a means of protecting the public against unscrupulous competitors. The surprising thing is that the public usually swallows this propaganda whole and fails to notice that licensing is effective principally in protecting existing producers from competition.[1]

It is not our intention here to construct a case against licensing per se—though candor compels the admission that we find the weight of the evidence heavily against using the power of the state to restrict entry in this fashion. The point which must be made is that competition is not effective in many areas of the economy precisely because the state has refused to permit competition. The consumer's best protection against exploitation by the seller of any good or service is the power of others to offer him a substitute. When the state limits the number of sellers or restricts the terms of exchange, it does so almost invariably in response to *industry* pressure; [2] and the most important if not the most apparent consequence is the reduction of competition.

The history of "fair trade" legislation provides another illuminating example of how competition can be eliminated in response to business pressures and ostensibly for the public welfare. The marketing revolution that began in retailing in the 1920s made available to consumers a wider variety of merchandise on more favorable terms. But the growth of chain stores, discount houses, and other efficient retailing outlets meant new and vigorous competition for many businessmen. Among their varied political responses were efforts to secure state-enforced minimum prices, of which "fair trade" laws are the best-known instance. Note the label that was applied: Laws to eliminate price competition or hobble innovations in an industry are presented to the public as laws aimed at creating "fair trade."

The competition which most industries find easiest to eliminate is competition from abroad. Laws that discriminate against foreign sellers injure domestic consumers by reducing the number of alternatives before them. But business firms have been very successful in securing government protection against foreign competition by perpetrating the myth that only foreigners are damaged through tariffs or quotas.

The obvious fact is that government—local, state, and Federal—is heavily involved in the creation and preservation of monopoly positions. Whether this can be justified in particular cases is another and more difficult question. But if we hope to acquire any perspective at all on the monopoly problem, we must begin by recognizing the extent to which monopoly is the creature of public policy. The government studiously restricts competition in major and minor industries, from broadcasting and barbering through transportation and veterinary medicine to agriculture and construction. It would be naïve to assume that this policy somehow works automatically for the welfare of consumers, especially in view of the passion for such controls displayed by the affected industries.

POPULAR MISCONCEPTIONS

Yet this is not what most people apparently have in mind when they express concern about the problem of monopoly power. They are thinking of General Motors, Standard Oil of New Jersey, and United States Steel—gigantic firms "dominating" their industries and, perhaps with the connivance of a few large cohorts, "administering" prices in accord with their own prejudiced notions of equity. Insofar as these people realize that monopoly power presupposes the ability to exclude competitors, they reason that sheer size is sufficient to accomplish this task.

But what are the advantages which size confers? And under what circumstances can these advantages be realized? A long list of negative statements must be recorded. Available evidence does not support the belief that the largest firms are the most efficient in every industry, nor that giantism is necessary for success even in industries dominated by giants, nor that large firms have acquired and maintained their dominant positions through predatory practices, nor that prices are higher in relation to costs in "oligopolistic" industries than in industries consisting of many small firms, nor that large firms have manipulated consumer demand rather than responding to it. All these generalizations are frequently put forward but rarely supported by any evidence. About the only generalization with regard to large firms that can be supported is that generalizations in this area are more misleading than revealing.

Significant monopoly power exists when a firm markets products for which good substitutes are not readily available. Whether this is true in any particular instance must be determined by a product analysis, not a firm analysis. If Du Pont enjoys excessive monopoly power in the sale of cellophane, this fact can be demonstrated only by examining the market for flexible wrapping products, not by looking at Du Pont's share of sales in the chemical industry. And when we have reached a conclusion with respect to cellophane, we have established nothing of significance with respect to Du Pont's position in the nylon market.

Procter & Gamble is a large enterprise, with total assets of more than one billion dollars. That says nothing about how much monopoly power P&G has in the detergent market.

Standard Oil of New Jersey has more than twelve billion dollars in assets. But how much freedom does that confer upon the company when the time comes for setting the price of its gasoline?

International Business Machines ranked ninth in sales among all industrial corporations in 1964. Is there any clear relation between that fact and the competition IBM faces in marketing any one of its products?

We do not intend to deny that size confers advantages. But the questions are where does it do so, to what extent, and with what consequences.

The notorious electrical conspiracy case, for example, provided dramatic evidence of competition as well as of collusion. General Electric and Westinghouse are the dominant firms in the electrical equipment industry, ranking fourth and fifteenth in sales among industrial corporations in the crucial year 1959. That they faced vigorous competition from one another and from other, much smaller firms is attested by the conspiracy itself. That relatively tiny firms could compete with the giants is proved by the fact that they were invited into the conspiracy. Allis-Chalmers was one-fifth the size of GE in 1959, Joslyn and Emerson were not even one-tenth the size of Allis Chalmers, and other participants in the conspiracy were smaller still.

The "meat packing trust" continues to be a favorite object of antimonopoly sentiment, as it has been at least since the beginning of the century. But the sentiment is unbelievably misdirected. For many years now there has been no Big Four (or Big Five) in the industry, returns on invested capital have been below average, and innovative newcomers have experienced little difficulty in getting themselves established in the industry.[3]

GENUINE AND RHETORICAL SOLUTIONS

But our argument with respect to the incidence and significance of monopoly is intended only to provide perspective on the problem, not to deny the phenomenon. Granted that the problem is neither as pervasive nor as serious as much discussion would have us believe, we are still left with the question of what to do about excessive market power where it exists.

In his April, 1962, attack on the steel price increase, President Kennedy stated that "steps are under way by those members of Congress who plan appropriate inquiries into . . . what legislative safeguards may be needed to protect the public interest." Abstracting from all questions as to whether or not legislative safeguards were needed in the case of steel, the President was here announcing a tenable policy. *If* some firms, acting singly or jointly, possess such substantial market power that they can do all of the harm to the national economy that the President alleged, it is intolerable that this power should be left in their hands. It is then the task of Congress to devise legislative safeguards for the public interest.

The President took another tack just a moment later. "Price and wage decisions," he asserted, ". . . are and ought to be freely and privately made. But the American people have a right to expect, in return for that freedom, a higher sense of business responsibility for the welfare of their country than has been shown in the last two days."

We submit that the American people have a right to expect something far different. If competition is not adequate to provide reasonable assurance that the freedom and power of businessmen will be exerted for the "welfare of their country," no sense of business responsibility, however high, will do as a substitute.

All the arguments of Chapter IV are again relevant here. No businessman, including the businessman with monopoly power, knows what the public interest requires. With the best intentions in the world he is simply not competent to sort out the public interest from the welter of conflicting demands made upon him. Corporate conscience has nothing to do with economizing, and it is economizing—the best possible use of society's resources—that we want from businessmen.

The appropriate response to monopoly is the promotion of competition, and if this proves impossible or inadequate, explicit regulations with all the sanctions of law are essential. This is a "hard saying," and it is apparently no more acceptable to businessmen than it is to many of their critics. That is certainly understandable. New laws or regulatory commissions and more vigorous competition restrict the freedom and power of the businessman, and no one likes to see his freedom or power diminished. The notion that businessmen "believe in" the virtues of a competitive economy is a half-truth at best. Many of them believe only in lower taxes, less government regulation of themselves, and weaker labor unions. Their true colors emerge when the time comes for government to intervene in their behalf; then a dismaying percentage of the business community proves how eager it is to abandon competition and free enterprise.

THE CURRENT RELEVANCE OF OLD BELIEFS

But if the faith is dying, it is not yet dead. Experiments behind the Iron Curtain with economizing by government directive may yet succeed in bringing home to skeptics the enormous advantages, both economic and political, of a decentralized economic system based on private property and controlled by free market competition.[4] But if these lessons are learned correctly, we shall not attempt to make a larger place for conscience in the economic system. We shall rather search continuously for ways to open closed markets and thus to reduce the extent and significance of monopoly power by promoting competition.

Perhaps the businessman holds out for conscience because he doubts that this last is a live option. Much of the rhetoric in the business community seems to assume that the only alternatives are social responsibility or government regulation, perhaps because businessmen have themselves failed to see how effectively competition continues to regulate the American economy.

This is not the place to construct a program for promoting economic competition. But a few ideas should already have suggested themselves. The withdrawal of present government support for monopoly could do much to enhance effective competition in many areas of the economy. Since every business merger tends to diminish the alternatives of buyers and suppliers, the present Federal policy of giving hostile scrutiny to proposed mergers has promise as a competition-preserving tactic. Collusion is another way of reducing competition, and while it cannot be prevented completely, vigorous enforcement of the Sherman Act seems to have made collusion a flimsy and fleeting foundation for monopoly power.

It would be odd and even tragic were we to give up on competition as a technique for the social control of business power when so much of the evidence points to its continued and growing effectiveness. The market power of businessmen is far less than we have been taught to believe. And where it does prove excessive, there are ways in which public policy can reinvigorate competition and thus bring that power under control. This will not always be easy. It will require attention to detail and to crucial differences. But even small steps in a constructive direction must be preferred to giant strides along a wrong or useless route.

Notes to Chapter VII.

[1] An interesting and instructive examination of the problem is Thomas G. Moore, "The Purpose of Licensing," *Journal of Law and Economics* (October, 1961), pp. 93–117.

[2] Recent research by Gabriel Kolko into the historical origins of "populist" and "progressive" reform measures strikingly confirms this thesis. See in particular his *Triumph of Conservatism* (The Free Press of Glencoe, New York, 1963), pp. 11–78.

[3] The trials of the meat packing industry have been recounted by Simon N. Whitney in *Antitrust Policies: American Experience in Twenty Industries,* vol. I (The Twentieth Century Fund, New York, 1958), pp. 27–94. His discussion provides an exemplary case

study in support of the thesis that the public will never allow its attitude toward "monopolists" to be modified by anything so trivial as the facts.

4 The recent economic reforms in the Soviet Union and its Eastern European satellites suggests that the moral has also been drawn by many of the central planners.

VIII.

Conscience and Injustice

In 1958, *Advertising Age* ran a feature article by Theodore Levitt entitled "Are Advertising and Marketing Corrupting Society? It's Not Your Worry, Levitt Tells Business." [1] The magazine's editors warned that it was a provocative article and one with which many readers would disagree. Subsequently, Raymond Baumhart, in his survey of business ethics in America, excerpted some sentences from Levitt's article and asked businessmen to comment on them:

> . . . the businessman exists for only one purpose, to create and deliver value satisfactions at a profit to himself. . . If what is offered can be sold at a profit (not even necessarily a long-term profit), then it is legitimate. . . . The cultural, spiritual, social, and moral consequences of his actions are none of his occupational concern.

"From top to bottom of the business ladder," Baumhart reported, "a convincing 94% say: 'We disagree.'" Most of his respondents, according to Baumhart, regarded untempered profit maximization as immoral. "Five out of every six executives in our survey reacted affirmatively to this . . . view: 'For corporation executives to act in the interest of shareholders alone, and not also in the interest of employees and consumers, is unethical.'" [2]

Some of the other evidence gleaned and reported by Baumhart casts doubt on his interpretation of these responses, but it seems safe to conclude that most businessmen would view the "cultural, spiritual, social, and moral consequences" of their actions as matters for legitimate "occupational concern." Is this, as so many assume today, grounds for ethical commendation? We instinctively think well of an individual who measures the broad consequences of his actions, and we are predisposed to commend the businessman who demonstrates a concern for "higher" values. Is it possible, however, that we are misleading ourselves?

There is no need to review here the economic case for profit maximization. We shall take it as established that maximum anticipated profit for the enterprise provides far and away the best single criterion for the businessman who wants to make decisions that will enhance the economic welfare of society. But economics is not the end of life; the efficient utilization of resources is primarily a means, a prerequisite of the good society and not that end itself. What should the businessman do when profit conflicts with other and perhaps more basic values? Should he pour waste directly into the river if this is cheaper than treating it? Should he erect a large and garish sign opposite a public park as long as this increases his net receipts? Should he give the American motorist useless and dangerous horsepower merely because the majority of motorists will pay more for this than for safety features on an automobile? Should he give up the idea of sponsoring fine drama and support a western instead when the marketing research people show that the latter provides more sales per dollar of television advertising expenditure?

Businessmen are uneasy about these questions because they suspect that the right answer is the unprofitable one in each case. No businessman of any sensitivity or refinement cares to pollute rivers, desecrate landscapes, promote automobile accidents, or corrupt public tastes. Some will simply refuse to do so, asserting that there is more to life than profit. Others will try to find a compromise for their consciences between profit and public duty as they perceive it. Still others will deny that they have the responsibilities implied and will go ahead with whatever looks most profitable. But none of the three groups has necessarily chosen the ethical course.

A WORLD OF GRAYS

Consider the river pollution example. If the cost of treating plant waste is so high that doing so will result in a serious deterioration of the firm's profit position, and if the firm's waste disposal actually makes no significant difference in the level of stream pollution, why is it unethical to pour untreated waste directly into the river?

A possible reply is that while one firm will make no real difference, serious pollution will result if all firms adopt the same attitude.

But how serious? Suppose the answer is very serious: Fish and vegetation will die, ugliness and stench will replace pastoral beauty, and downstream communities will be put to heavy expense to purify their drinking water.

Yet if all these grave consequences are to be expected from businessmen's failure to control industrial wastes, ought such control be left to the ethical sense of individual businessmen? Not only does this provide no assurance that the public interest in an unpolluted river will be protected; it places individual businessmen in a position where they must make decisions that they are not competent to make.

Why are they not competent? Because the businessman is being told to choose between a polluted and an unpolluted river, but in fact he does not have this choice. He can only choose between contributing or not contributing toward pollution, and that is far from the same thing. The New York City motorist who buys an afterburner for his automobile does contribute toward cleaner air in the community; but he is in no way competent to decide for or against smog by *his* actions. He is therefore being sensible, not unethical, when he refuses to incur the expense of the afterburner.

A decision against stream or air pollution must be a collective decision because it requires simultaneous action on the part of many people. It is therefore properly a *political* decision. It is up to the legislature or some other appropriate political body to determine the public interest and establish the appropriate sanctions. When we cast this burden upon the businessman's conscience, we are being just neither to the public nor to the businessman.

WHOSE RESPONSIBILITY?

As another example, consider the problem of automobile design. Automobile manufacturers have long been scolded for adding fins, chrome, gadgets, and horsepower while neglecting economy of purchase and operation, durability, and, above all, safety. After the 1966 congressional hearings on automobile safety, politicians and editorial writers joined in lamenting Detroit's failure to clean its own house, a failure that now made government action imperative.

But why did Detroit fail to clean house? Note first of all that "Detroit" is misleading, implying a single decision center on questions of automobile design. The manufacturers actually decide these questions singly and would run a serious risk of antitrust prosecution if they did not. So the question must be put more accurately: Why did General Motors, Ford, and Chrysler continue to stress trivial and even dangerous features in automobile design to the relative neglect of such vital matters as safety?

The question can readily be answered. To the extent that they did so, the automobile manufacturers sacrificed safety to horsepower and frills in the belief that this would maximize their profits. They doubted that the public was much interested in safe and ugly cars; they were reasonably sure the public would pay for dash and glamor. There is little evidence that they were wrong in this judgment. The phenomenon of the Volkswagen, far from proving that Americans would reject the Detroit designs given a chance, shows that a large majority of us are willing to pay a steep price for dash and glamor in our transportation. (The Checker automobile is further evidence.) It would be strange indeed if the men in the automobile industry did seriously misread public demand for long. They have the strongest incentives not to do so.

But should the manufacturers have built and sold safety despite public indifference? This is what many have maintained; and this was supposedly the ethical or socially responsible course. But why is it ethical for a firm to provide its customers with something that they like *less?* Because it's better for the customers, of course. But why is a manufacturer more competent than his customers to decide what is in their best interest?

Moreover, even if we all agreed that safety is better than glamor, we would not have moved one step closer to deciding the actual issue: How much safety do we want at what cost in terms of glamor? *That* is the decision the designers faced, not a decision between safety and glamor. The choices they actually made, based on their reading of demand, were calculated to maximize profits. But they were simultaneously humble decisions, a fact that critics of the automobile industry have too often overlooked.

For when a manufacturer imposes his own values, tastes, or preferences upon his customers, he not only runs the risk of losing out to a competitor more eager to please; he also assumes that his values, tastes, and preferences are better than his customers'. Perhaps he is right. But who is to say? And such a claim, too often advanced, will earn a reputation for arrogance, not social responsibility.

There is nothing at all tragic about the fact that the automobile industry failed to act and thus made government intervention necessary. If there is a discernible public interest in safer automobiles, so that the verdict of the market is not socially acceptable, then it is the task of government to define that interest and secure it with appropriate sanctions. When private businessmen assume this responsibility, they are shouldering a task for which they have neither the vocation nor the competence. Viewed from one standpoint, such behavior is arrogant; from another, it is simply ineffective because the public will buy what it prefers from those willing to comply with its preferences. No matter how we view it, it is not obviously "ethical."

RESPONSIBILITY OR USURPATION?

Much has been written in recent years about the responsibility of the businessman with regard to the problems of civil rights. The hiring procedures of business firms have caused them to be lauded as pioneers and decried as reactionaries, but whatever the verdict on their performance it has been generally agreed that businessmen have ethical obligations in this area. But here again, as it turns out, the issue is by no means so clear as we have pretended.

Most business firms have discriminated against Negroes in the past, and many continue to do so. Some of the tragic consequences of this participation by business in community patterns of prejudice are now emerging so clearly that all can see them; "liberal" Northerners, long accustomed to denounce the South for its treatment of the Negro, have been compelled to admit that discrimination in employment as practiced in the North may be more urbane but is no less vicious in its effect than the "customs" of the South. What is to be done?

Some civil rights leaders have urged reverse discrimination as a means of compensating for past mistreatment of the Negro. This recommendation has been sympathetically received in some business circles, loudly rejected in others, and quietly ignored in most. What would be the ethical response to such a demand?

There is no easy way to decide. We sometimes overlook the fact that discrimination affects a race by affecting individuals and that attempts to rectify past wrongs are for this reason alone not really possible. The Negro who was forced by prejudice into a menial job thirty years ago is not compensated by attractive employment offers to young Negroes today. Moreover, reverse discrimination as it is usually proposed does not really require Caucasians to atone for their past mistreatment of the Negro. The businessman who passes over an eligible Caucasian in order to promote a less eligible Negro may suppose that he is engaged in an act of racial penance; in fact, he is doing no penance because he is not bearing the burden. It is a strange notion of guilt and penance that would allow white people to suppose they have atoned for past wrongs when they have begun to discriminate against selected Caucasians. The Caucasian passed over in favor of the Negro may well wonder at the virtue of a system which makes him the scapegoat for a long history of social wrongs.

We are in no way trying to minimize the evils which past and present discriminations have created. And we are strongly persuaded that positive measures must now be taken to ameliorate the glaring inequities in our society that discrimination has left as a legacy. But insofar as it is a social problem, it is not a problem which the businessman is particularly competent to handle.

The fact that many businessmen will dissent from this position does not prove that they are ethical. Might they not be dissenting, and might other Caucasians not be joining them, because they recognize that business action to correct past wrongs can confine the burden to selected groups in society? When an employer hires a Negro over a Caucasian, perhaps he buys an easy conscience; but the employee pays the bill. Few businessmen are happy over such a prospect as A. Philip Randolph's proposed 100-billion-dollar war on racial injustice, for it will have costs that they do not wish to bear. But whatever the demerits of such proposals, they have the distinct merit of attacking a *social* problem by political means. As an individual, the businessman may certainly accept an ethical obligation to incur personal sacrifices in behalf of those who have been discriminated against. But this is another matter entirely and, incidentally, an approach that enjoys far less acceptance among businessmen.

It may be that the horrible legacy of racial injustice can only be eliminated through social surgery. Such surgery will be painful for many; but that is precisely why it must be performed through political processes and not by the scalpel of self-appointed surgeons in the business community.

THE AMBIGUITIES OF SOCIAL JUSTICE

The undeniable fact is that many businessmen *have* made "the cultural, spiritual, social, and moral consequences" of their actions a matter of occupational concern. Moreover, they have engaged in a considerable amount of propaganda activity to convince the rest of us that these values will be best cared for by the business community. This was no doubt inevitable. But we are not required to accept it as an ethical or politically tolerable program. For it is finally not the vocation of the businessman to be the shepherd and guardian of these values; and if he claims such a role for himself, other voices must be raised to accuse him of pretension and arrogance. It is the job of the businessman to maximize the anticipated profits of his enterprise and thereby to fulfill his part in the enormously important task of allocating society's resources. This is a worthy and demanding vocation. But it confers no special call to be society's prophet, priest, or king.

Social justice is the amorphous but alluring goal that floats before us when we begin to urge upon the businessman acceptance of his social responsibilities. But the moment that we utter such a demand, we have begun to endorse actual injustice. It is essential that we see in what sense this is so. And to do this, we must detour briefly through some abstract terrain.

Justice and power are indissolubly connected. We have already asserted that mankind's continuing search for social justice is at root an inquiry into the problem of power: its nature, its uses, and its distribution. It is widely recognized that justice is unlikely in the absence of an appropriate distribution of power. But we have been slow to see that justice is impossible under such circumstances.

Justice is, of course, a difficult concept to define, so difficult, in fact, that many have come to regard use of the word as a mere rhetorical device. And there can be little doubt that the word is as often used to beg questions as to answer them. Nonetheless, we do talk about justice, we entertain it as an ideal, and we expend a great deal of effort in what we call the pursuit of justice. All this activity is surely "about" something.

Much of our confusion arises from a failure to recognize

explicitly what we all concede implicitly: that an absolute and a relative element are both always present in the concept of justice. When we insist that what is just in a given instance depends upon the facts of the particular situation, we are calling attention to the relative element. But when we deny that justice is merely what people *think* is just or assert that a situation can be unjust even though a majority of people hold it to be just, we are appealing to the absolute element. This fundamental and unavoidable polarity must be taken into account if we are to engage in a meaningful discussion of justice and avoid the twin dangers of a sterile relativism and an irrelevant dogmatism.

Justice requires basically that each receive his due. This is the most general and inclusive meaning which the concept possesses for us. That this does not require perfect equality of treatment is proved by our refusal to concede that what is in justice due to an adult is also in justice due to a child. What is due to anyone depends upon what that person *is:* In the language of perennial philosophy, it is dependent upon his *being*. The claim of everyone for justice is rooted in his being, and that which is due him must be in proportion to his power of being.

JUSTICE AND POWER

This sounds vague, and in a sense it is, for it is an attempt to state in words the most general form of justice, or what it is to which we ultimately refer when we make an appeal to justice. We cannot expect easy answers to one of the most persistent and perplexing problems in human thought. But our definition is not arbitrary, at least not in intention. We are asserting that this is what we ultimately mean when we employ the concept of justice as a norm which judges relations among men.

If a father were to treat his five-year-old son as an equal, he would be unjust to the child (as well as to himself), for he would be treating the child as something more than what he is. If, on the other hand, he denied the child any rights at all and made his own being the criterion of all behavior toward the child, he would again be behaving unjustly.

A highly competent person is in justice due more than a less competent person: Not everyone has a "right" to be President of the United States or president of a large corporation or even president of the local PTA. A person with a powerful personality is in justice due something different from what is due to a timid or uncertain person. The student with more academic potential is in justice entitled to a larger scholarship than the student with little potential.

The criterion of being or power of being is not arbitrary; but it is always ambiguous. It exists as a meaningful norm, but its implications are difficult to discern. It follows that injustice in the name of justice is an ever-present possibility. It is in fact such a familiar phenomenon to all of us that we must take into account yet another relation between power and justice.

BALANCE OF POWER AND JUSTICE

We are in the habit of speaking of the *demand* for justice, even in situations where no verbal demand has been formulated. This is more than a mere way of speaking. If a person's *power to be* is the norm determining what he is due, it makes sense to speak of a demand in the sense in which power does demand. When a demand arises out of actual power, it carries its own imperative; this is what we somehow recognize when we speak of the demands or the obligations of justice. In fact, there can be no such thing as a demand for justice in the absence of power to support it.

Balance-of-power politics has been unfairly derided by moralists who have failed to see this intimate relation between power and justice. Unless it is rooted in actual power, the demand for justice degenerates into a pitiable plea—and a plea that is actually for injustice—for *more* than is due. As someone once observed, it is tyrannical on the part of the lamb to demand that the lion lie down beside it: This asks him to cease being a lion. It is unjust for those without power to receive the same rights and responsibilities as those with substantial power, and no society, small or large, can long endure such injustice.

The assertion by some civil rights leaders in 1966 that the Negro's demand for justice now had to give way to a quest for power was a fundamentally misleading claim. Without power the Negro will not receive justice, as the long history of nations certainly demonstrates. Even more basically, what is in justice due to the Negro—to the race and to the individual—must be determined with reference to the power that he possesses.

Might does make right. This is not an immoral piece of cynicism but a profound truth of both politics and ethics. Viewed from the political standpoint, powerlessness on the part of an individual or group allows its rights to be determined completely by others. And those rights will be progressively whittled away. A defenseless nation loses territory, wealth, population, the loyalty of its citizens, and finally its existence. A social organization without power may make claims for itself but will be without rights and will continue to exist only so long as it is tolerated. An individual without power (no person who is alive is *completely* devoid of power) must continually yield to the demands of others.

Moreover, this process cannot be checked by an appeal to justice because the demand for justice is ultimately rooted in the power of the individual or group making the appeal.

Might *defines* right, both politically and ethically. Any other attempted ground for right and justice will prove arbitrary, unsuccessful, and therefore unjust.

Most of the objections which we instinctively raise against the contention that might makes right derive from a superficial notion of might. Power has more adequate connotations, and it is the word we prefer to use. Everything that exists has power or it would not exist. The power which people possess, for example, is partially revealed in every human encounter—as personality, vital force, influence, persuasiveness, authority, command over persons and things, all of which we attempt to summarize in the single phrase "power of being." And it is to this power that we look when we attempt to decide what justice requires in any situation.

How does all of this bear upon the problem before us? In what sense can we now say that it is actually *un*just to ask that justice be dispensed according to the dictates of the businessman's conscience?

The primary assertion we can make is that justice is not a dole; it is a demand. Justice is not a matter of privilege, but of right. If the businessman possesses such extraordinary social power that we have no choice but to throw ourselves upon his mercy, he is a despot. And the administrations of a despot, however benevolent, are not justice. If the social power of any businessman is so unchecked that he is able by his decisions to choose for his society between great good and great evil, justice demands first of all that this power be brought under control. The failure to do so will ensure injustice, for despotism is inherently unjust and is rarely benevolent for long.

Imperialism, or the attempt to acquire disproportionate power at the expense of others, is so familiar and obvious a tendency in social life that it could almost be called a law. Hostility toward disproportionate power and toward all attempts to aggrandize power is therefore a basic prerequisite of any serious quest for social justice. The entire political tradition of the United States affirms this central proposition. And there is no good reason for confining its application to the phenomenon of governmental power. If the businessman is genuinely determined to use his power, the power to organize economic resources efficiently, to make himself the arbiter of cultural, spiritual, social, or moral values, he is an imperialist. And he must be resisted, not encouraged and applauded, in the name of justice.

But there is even more than can now be said. Is the businessman really as eager to occupy this position as some are currently pretending? The businessman possesses no peculiar capacities or special insights for choosing among competing cultural, spiritual, social, and moral values. If it is unjust to demand of anyone that which is beyond his power, it is unjust to impose upon the businessman responsibilities which he is essentially incapable of fulfilling. Responsibility without power is an onerous burden; the businessman has every right to protest against such an unwarranted imposition.

As for the businessman who gladly accepts these extraordinary responsibilities, is he not finally unjust to himself? Power tends to corrupt the wielder of power, and absolute power corrupts absolutely. Taken seriously, the doctrine of social responsibility fosters megalomania in its adherents. It places upon the businessman's conscience intolerable burdens that tempt him continually to arrogance and pharisaism.

The businessman who begins to perceive all of this will not seek or claim for himself an elite position in society. He will rather join in insisting that positive checks and balances be erected against every manifestation of social power and that responsibility for the public good remain a matter of public concern.

Notes to Chapter VIII.

[1] Theodore Levitt, "Are Advertising and Marketing Corrupting Society? It's Not Your Worry, Levitt Tells Business," *Advertising Age* (Oct. 6, 1958).

[2] Raymond C. Baumhart, "How Ethical Are Businessmen?" *Harvard Business Review* (July–August, 1961), pp. 8, 10. Baumhart rearranges, without changing the sense, remarks made by Levitt in *op. cit.*, p. 89.

IX.

The Ethical Businessman

W ar," as Talleyrand supposedly said, "is much too serious a thing to be left to military men." And the control of a society's economic system is much too serious a thing to be left to businessmen. Businessmen are the generals (and lesser officers), but policy must be made by civilians.

We seem to be bent, however, on reversing that relationship. The businessman is widely distrusted in our society when he is tending to the task he knows well, which is the organization of resources in a manner best calculated to yield a maximum profit for the businessman and an efficient allocation for society. When he deserts his post, however, and sets himself up as some kind of social dictator, he is suddenly rewarded with looks of warm approbation. We are unwilling to believe that the businessman is doing an effective job at that which he knows best; but we are willing and even eager to assign him much broader responsibilities.

At the root of this confused approach is probably our inability to appreciate the way in which a market economy operates. Competition and free enterprise are officially venerated among us, but our piety is razor-thin for all the ardor of its expression. We just do not believe that the market effectively regulates and controls the activities of businessmen. If the public good is to be secured, it must be consciously and directly promoted. And we have asked businessmen to play the leading part by recognizing and accepting their social responsibilities.

But why is the businessman today so eager to accept this invitation? We cannot overlook the fact that businessmen have been among the most strident proclaimers of the new social gospel, that they have been major contributors to the literature and philosophy of social responsibility, and that with near unanimity they have announced their willingness to bear this burden. Public relations and image making are a large part of the answer, of course. Businessmen are aware of the hostility and suspicion with which their activities are viewed, and the managers of large business firms in particular know that valuable goodwill can often be purchased with a few cents' worth of pious profession. To some extent we are playing an elaborate game in which talk is a substitute for action.

But there must be more to the matter than this. The doctrine of social responsibility is ardently held by many smaller businessmen for whom the public relations effect is inconsequential, and the managers of large enterprises will often maintain their position even more vigorously off the record than on. The conclusion seems inescapable that businessmen *want* to have social responsibilities, that they genuinely reject profit maximization as the goal of business activity, and that "the cultural, spiritual, social, and moral consequences" of their actions are close to their hearts.

For Raymond Baumhart and many others, this is proof that the level of ethical ideals is rising in the business community. But it may be an indication of something totally different and not at all reassuring. Today's businessman may be suffering from profound status anxiety, and his thinking in this area may grow out of a desperate desire for self-justification.

AN UNCONVENTIONAL THESIS

In a way, there would be nothing novel or unusual about this. Men have been concerned with the problem of justification since the beginning of history. When Adam placed the blame on Eve and Eve passed it on to the serpent, they were behaving in a fashion we have all come to recognize as distinctively human. Each of us wants to be justified before whatever "gods" he acknowledges, to know that he merits approval, to possess that inner assurance which accompanies a sense of personal worth. The businessman is no different from the rest of us.

But the businessman today may have a particularly hard time of it. Somehow the suspicion has grown within the business community that business itself badly needs justification. Another way of putting it would be to say that businessmen are no longer as sure as they once were about the meaning and value of what they are doing.

In recent years there has been a great deal of interest in the phenomenon of business ideology, much of it sparked by Francis Sutton's *The American Business Creed*.[1] But why should the businessman need an ideology? What function does it serve?

Ideology is self-justification by creed and slogan. It is a way of thinking about oneself or one's group, a set of beliefs that justify what one is or does. Ideology is not necessarily false. In fact, if it is too inconsistent with reality, it won't work. It operates not so much by falsifying reality as by distorting it, playing up certain elements and playing down others, with the net result that an image is created which can sustain and support the person holding the ideology. We all have ideologies, of course; but sometimes they get out of hand. Sometimes they cease merely to support and begin taking over. This could be a symptom of profound status anxiety.

Whenever any group in society starts talking about the need to project or perfect its image, sell the public on the importance of its role, or become "a true profession," that group is displaying the classic symptoms of status anxiety.[2] And status anxiety is just one strain, albeit a relatively new one, of an ancient form of virus: the desperate human craving for self-justification.

An exaggerated statement of the thesis will at least make the point unmistakably clear: When businessmen today begin to talk about the necessity for accepting their social responsibilities, or express an interest in discussing business ethics, or form a committee to draft an ethical code for their industry, they are not so much looking for ethical guidance in decision making as they are looking for self-justification. Business seminars on ethics and social responsibility are thus a kind of neurosis.

Now psychologists tell us that a neurosis can be a very useful thing. A neurosis arises because a person cannot fully face some unacceptable reality. The neurosis is, in a sense, the cure for the unacceptable reality. A good neurosis works: It permits the neurotic to function. It allays his anxiety and allows him to get on with the tasks of life, whatever they may be.

We are not claiming, of course, that all businessmen are neurotics. In any event, there is a little bit of the neurotic in all of us. Moreover, the particular neurosis of which we are speaking is hardly confined to businessmen. The disease may be especially virulent, for example, among college professors. For the college professor knows that he is an exceptionally important member of society; yet society ignores him most of the time. It calls his intelligent, well-thought-out, carefully documented, and invariably profound opinions "ivory tower stuff." It kindly, but smugly, refers to him as an egghead. Society acts as if importance were measured by income, and despite rising academic salaries of recent years, college professors still deem themselves woefully underpaid by contrast with business executives and others whom the professor deems his peers at best and probably his inferiors. And so college faculties spawn all sorts of interesting neuroses. And long-suffering students have often been compelled to endure lectures designed not so much to educate the student as to justify the professor. The present argument should not be construed, therefore, as another instance of academic sniping at the businessman.

Moreover, the desire for self-justification is not all bad. It can be the beginning of the examined life, the only kind of life that many wise men have deemed worth living. It can be evidence, too, of a moral earnestness without which no society can long endure and without which a good society is utterly impossible. Self-doubt is the beginning of all doubt, and doubt is still the beginning of knowledge. It is above all the beginning of self-knowledge. And self-knowledge is a very great good indeed.

But the opportunity may be too lightly tossed away. It is temptingly easy, when businessmen start asking ethical questions, to hand them ethical answers on a platter—or a wall plaque. This will not do at all. The true goal of ethical inquiry must be something far deeper. For serious ethical questions simply do not admit of the kind of answer for which businessmen appear to be looking. An ethical rule never actually resolves an ethical dilemma (though it may provide the questioner with an excuse for doing what he has already determined to do.) For the good, which is the central concern of ethics, is finally what a good man does. Being ethical is, after all, just that: a matter of *being*. The prob-

lem before the businessman who aspires to be ethical is not
that of doing, but of becoming and being. And with this in-
troduction we are prepared, at long last, to say a good word
for ethics.

ETHICS FROM ANOTHER PERSPECTIVE

In one way or another, the entire argument so far has been a
sustained assault upon ethics or, more accurately, upon a particular misconception of the nature and function of ethics.
But that is because we have been unethical in demanding
too much and too little from ethics. We have unfairly applied
to the businessman's conduct a standard which he cannot
meet, and have obscured his genuine duties with tiresome
cant about his social responsibilities. On the other side of
the coin, we have abandoned the public interest in such matters as monopoly power or stream and air pollution by pretending that the enlightened conscience of the businessman
is capable of resolving such problems. Individual ethics is
not capable of solving economic or political problems, and it
is unjust to society to pretend otherwise.

But we have also demanded too little from ethics. We
have assumed that ethical rules make ethical men, or at least
that ethical conduct can be secured by the enunciation of
ethical rules. And we have thereby diverted the attention of
businessmen from what is the genuinely ethical problem: the
problem of becoming an ethical man.

The good is what a good man does! But what, exactly,
does a good man do? This is the question which persistently
recurs. There is finally only one way to answer this question:
Find a good man, and *see* what he does. This is not a trivial
or mocking answer. It is an earnest and important answer
because it calls attention to the two most important facets
of the general problem of ethics in business and all of life.[3]

In the first place, it is simply impossible to lay down in

advance a set of behavioral rules that will differentiate right from wrong in even a significant fraction of the ethical dilemmas businessmen actually encounter. Every situation is unique. Theorists are inclined to forget this fact, but those who must act are continually reminded. Every situation therefore requires a new decision. An *ethical* decision will be made only by an ethical man who knows the situation, discerns what ought to be done, and does it. Those who persist in the belief that if only certain rules are obeyed, we shall have ethical conduct in business are much too abstract about ethics, far too disrespectful toward the particular and the concrete, naïve in their failure to recognize the rationalizing talent with which each of us can escape an onerous rule, and doomed to continual frustration of their expectations.

The other facet to which this answer calls attention (find a good man, and *see* what he does) is this: Becoming ethical is a matter of becoming, of a change in being. Our basic ethical concern ought not to be with what businessmen do but with what they are. In the last analysis any serious inquiry into business ethics comes down to these questions: Who is the businessman? What ought he to be? And what are his resources for becoming what he ought to be?

THE QUEST FOR THE ETHICAL BUSINESSMAN

Now we are swimming (and hopefully, not floundering) in deep water. But ethics just is deep water, and if we wanted to remain in a wading pool we should have confined ourselves to something simple, like linear programming. A writer for the *Harvard Business Review* struck to the heart of the issue a few years back, in an article that most readers probably failed even to recognize as a discussion of business ethics. The article was entitled "The Importance of Being Human." [4] Here is our most urgent need: *men in business who are fully human.* If an ethical businessman has to be defined, we would define him simply as a man in business who is the full measure of what a man should be.

No serious ethical inquiry can escape the question of what it means to be human. What is "the nature and destiny of man," to use Reinhold Niebuhr's phrase? When is a "man for himself," as Erich Fromm puts the question? How does a man become "autonomous" in David Riesman's sense of the word? What is man essentially, to use the language of Paul Tillich and perennial philosophy? All these are different ways of asking the same question, the fundamental question for all of ethics.

It is obvious that no comprehensive answer can be given here, much less an answer that will satisfy each reader. What follows will inevitably partake of the nature of personal confession as much as rational argument. But it is put forward more to elicit the reader's own reflections than to secure his detailed assent.

THE NATURE OF MAN

Man is freedom. This must be said first of all. If man is not free, ethical inquiry, indeed all inquiry, is a waste of time grounded in an illusion, and there is nothing that is human about man. We know that we are free because our freedom weighs upon us. We can *choose*. We can come to the fork in the road, the moment of decision: We can weigh, consider, and *decide*. We know that we bear responsibility for what we do; this is the meaning of remorse, of guilt, of repentance, of renewed determination. And where there is responsibility, there is freedom. Responsibility comes from the Latin *respondere*, "to answer." We must answer the world in which we live and which we daily encounter, and above all the people among whom we live and whom we encounter. We could not answer if we did not have freedom; we could only react. But we know that we can and must answer. And this is both the glory and the risk of being human.

But man's freedom is not unlimited. We are finite creatures, possessed from birth of a history and hence of a destiny that we did not create. We are "thrown into" existence, to swim and sometimes to sink, and the depth of the water is not a matter of our own choosing. We cannot make the world over. We cannot have it all the way we would like it. We are compelled always to work with the refractory and sometimes unmanageable stuff that has been assigned to us at the place where we have been planted.

Our freedom makes us creators; but our destiny reminds us that we are simultaneously creatures. To be truly human is to live at one and the same time as creature and creator. An ethical man, a good man, a man who is fully human, will not surrender his creativity in passive submission to what is, nor deny his creatureliness by claiming to be more than he is.

Know thyself. This is the beginning of virtue as well as of wisdom. The virtuous or good man knows himself for what he is and neither deprecates himself unfairly nor entertains delusions of grandeur. He is a humble man, as becomes a creature, but simultaneously a proud man as benefits a creator. He possesses self-respect, the basis of all respect for others, without self-obsession, which excludes genuine respect for others. He is humane because he is human and because he knows and respects his own humanity.

THE TEMPTATIONS OF THE BUSINESSMAN

The situation of the businessman is just a special instance of the human situation, and no temptation befalls him which is not common to man. The requirements of "the system," with their insistent demands, continually urge him to surrender his integrity and to find success, meaning, an approval in the rewards and marks of accomplishment which "the system" doles out. If he is in business for himself, he is tempted to regard the profitability of his enterprise as proof not just of his business skills but of his worth as a man. If he works for a corporation, he is tempted to look to the corporation as the source of every good, to locate in "the organization" rather than in himself the standards and the judgments by which he lives.

When this fails to work, when his self-abandonment proves unable to provide the satisfaction for which he is looking, he is tempted in the opposite direction. He wonders whether his work has any meaning at all and feels trapped in his position. Then he readily begins to ignore his limitations and the boundaries of his situation, to abandon his concrete responsibilities for delusions of omnicompetence. It is in such moments that he is most tempted by the vanities of "social responsibility."

The plight of the businessman is not made easier by the unwarranted attacks upon business that issue today from so many quarters. All that is wrong with our society is thoughtlessly laid at the doorstep of business. Business itself is implicitly defined as the ordinary, unimportant, and even sordid side of life. Inflation is attributed to profiteering, technological unemployment is laid to the businessman's ruthlessness, and much that is ugly in our society is blamed on his greed. As we argued extensively in Chapter III, the businessman has been the unfortunate victim of superficial thinking and careless speaking. Business has been made the scapegoat for society's ills, even by many who would deem themselves probusiness. We have widely failed to recognize that the businessman is society's principal architect of rationality, the creator not, indeed, of civilization but of the possibility of civilization. We have not allowed ourselves to see that the economical use of resources is a challenging task, a task of utmost importance to society, and a task that offers wide opportunities for the exercise of creative imagination. The businessman has begun to believe the libels that are written about him and to lose all confidence, as we asserted earlier, in the meaning and value of what he is doing.

BEGINNING AGAIN

The businessman concerned about ethics might do well to begin, therefore, with a long and careful look at the actual nature of the broad enterprise in which he is engaged. Without undue defensiveness, he must examine the varied charges brought against him. While rejecting some portions of the indictment, he may discover that business is vulnerable on other counts. He will want to ask, for example, to what extent businessmen have been myopic in talking about the national interest. While it is not the task of the businessman as businessman directly to promote the public good, he has often seized the initiative in defining it. Chambers of commerce and other businessmen's associations have been surprisingly successful in identifying human welfare with output, jobs, and monetary income. They have muddied public discussion of such problems as zoning, billboard control, local tax policies, and trade regulation in general by assuming and persuading others to assume that gross national product is the only public good and each community's share in it the only rational goal for policy. The businessman is certainly able to contribute something better than this to democratic discussion of the public good.

But the businessman will probably not be able to look honestly and without undue defensiveness at his place and role in society unless he first gains an understanding of business itself. Everything that was said in Chapter III by way of offering a more adequate definition of business is incorporated by reference here. The businessman must see from the outset the vacuity and irrelevance of the common canards which make business activity a low and unworthy form of human behavior.

Economizing activity is creative activity. The organization of resources, the deployment of men and materials, the estimation and manipulation of uncertain and shifting variables—all in such a manner as to maximize the value attainable—are a vocation worthy of anyone equal to it. It can be mere time-serving, of course, as well as dull, humdrum, useless. But so can any other occupation.

ENTHUSIASM AND THE ETHICAL MAN

The continuing debate which Joseph Schumpeter initiated a quarter century ago [5] on whether the spirit of enterprise is dying in our society often misses the point. If enterprise has in fact become routinized, bureaucratized—and the charge has not been established—the real danger is that a large and growing proportion of our creative people will find their principal work dull, tasteless, and unsatisfying, The monetary rewards will not compensate for the loss of joy in one's work.

Production is not merely for the sake of consumption. It is—or ought to be—in some sense worth doing for its own sake. Man as creator is summoned to rule over the earth and subdue it, and in the process of doing so he fulfills himself as well as creating things to eat, drink, ride in, or lounge upon.

This must not be interpreted as an endorsement of the Puritan Gospel of Work. The "busyness" with which so many Americans bustle around, *making* work for themselves to do, is a symptom of frustration and not a sign of creativity. Perhaps the essential difference is that the Puritan does not subdue his work but is subdued by it because he feels that he can be justified only by his accomplishments. This is not at all what we are urging. The sense of guilt, of worthlessness, of meaninglessness that drives so many of us so often and probably all of us some of the time may be conducive to great technical achievements, but it will not result in great human achievement. There is a real and profound difference, however hard it may be at times to discern it, between the man who drives himself and the man who is driven by his work.

Alfred North Whitehead's 1927 address to the American Association of the Collegiate Schools of Business should be read aloud annually to the faculties of such schools and to the students who are enrolling in them in ever-mounting numbers.[6] "So far as the mere imparting of information is concerned," Whitehead observed, "no university has had any justification for existence since the popularization of printing in the fifteenth century. . . . The justification for a university is that it preserves the connection between knowledge and the zest of life." Whitehead unflinchingly applied this point to business and education for business: "The main function of such a school is to produce men with a greater zest for business." Whitehead refused to accept the "libel upon human nature . . . that zest for life is the product of pedestrian purposes directed toward the narrow routine of material comforts." But Whitehead saw modern business as intellectual adventure, and his words have become no less true in the intervening forty years.

> In the complex organisations of modern business the intellectual adventure of analysis, and of imaginative reconstruction, must precede any successful reorganisation. . . . Today business organisation requires an imaginative grasp of the psychologies of populations engaged in differing modes of occupation; of populations scattered through cities, through mountains, through plains; of populations on the ocean, and of populations in mines, and of populations in forests. It requires an imaginative grasp of conditions in the tropics, and of conditions in temperate zones. It requires an imaginative grasp of the interlocking interests of great organisations, and of the reactions of the whole complex to any change in one of its elements. It requires an imaginative understanding of laws of political economy, not merely in the abstract, but also with the power to construe them in terms of the particular

circumstances of a concrete business. It requires some knowledge of the habits of government, and of the variations of those habits under diverse conditions. It requires an imaginative vision of the binding forces of any human organisation, a sympathetic vision of the limits of human nature and of the conditions which evoke loyalty of service. It requires some knowledge of the laws of health, and of the laws of fatigue, and of the conditions for sustained reliability. It requires an imaginative understanding of the social effects of the conditions of factories. It requires a sufficient conception of the role of applied science in modern society. It requires that discipline of character which can say "yes" and "no" to other men, not by reason of blind obstinacy, but with firmness derived from a conscious evaluation of relevant alternatives.[7]

Business can be exciting; it can arouse the zest of the businessman because of the numerous and varied opportunities which it provides for imaginative blending of the concrete and the universal. Every business firm and every decision maker within a firm faces a unique set of particulars that can never be wholly mastered by general rules. And these particulars are continually shifting in novel ways. The challenge before the businessman is the imaginative exploitation of these possibilities. And the formal principle which guides and appraises his work is profit on invested capital, the common denominator of business activity.

Business is not busy-ness, and zest does not imply mindless activism. The businessman of whom we are speaking will find time to stand back from his work, the way a painter stands back from his easel. He will reflect upon his achievements, but always remembering that the greatest achievement of a man is to become the full measure of his own potentiality.

OLD TRUTHS FOR A NEW ERA

All that we have been trying to say in the last few pages turns out to be a restatement of some very ancient ideas. We shall summarize them in quite traditional language, leaving it to the reader to decide whether the tradition is tired or vital.

The language and the traditions are theological. But this is not unprecedented in ethical discussion. To be fully human, the businessman must accept with enthusiasm the world that has come into his hands; he must receive all things with thanksgiving. Secondly, he must fashion that world free from the corroding influence of anxiety and guilt; he must live by grace. Finally, he must respond to everything and every person he encounters with full respect for what they are; and this is what the theologians call love.

Such a man, though he may agonize, will finally know what to do when confronted by an ethical dilemma, and will do it.

It is open to the reader to object that all of this is hopeless utopianism, that we have transformed a simple question about business ethics and social responsibility into a call for some kind of conversion or personal transformation. Perhaps so. But if businessmen are not such men as this, it is certain that no pious public pronouncements, no formulas for social responsibility, no industry codes or rules for fair practice, no brave ethical principles will make a noticeable difference. For the ethical life is the good life, and only a good man will be able to live it.

Notes to Chapter IX.

1 Francis X. Sutton et al., *The American Business Creed* (Harvard University Press, Cambridge, Mass., 1956; Schocken Paperback, 1962).

2 For a choice illustration from an industry much given to this kind of thing, see "Admen Pine for a Shinier Image," *Business Week* (May 5, 1962), pp. 49–50. The "advertising of advertising" with which we have all become familiar is a further symptom.

[3] If anyone were to infer from this that an individual can decide what he should do merely by imitating another individual, he would have misinterpreted the argument completely. But since this misunderstanding has cropped up in the writer's discussions with businessmen, it may be wise to point out explicitly that by observing an ethical businessman, we can learn only what *one* ethical businessman will do in *one unique* situation.

[4] Alvin Pitcher, "The Importance of Being Human," *Harvard Business Review* (January–February, 1961), pp. 41–48.

[5] Joseph A. Schumpeter, *Capitalism, Socialism, and Democracy* (Harper Torchbooks, Harper & Row, Publishers, Incorporated, New York, 1962), pp. 131–134.

[6] Alfred North Whitehead, "Universities and Their Function," in *The Aims of Education and Other Essays* (The Macmillan Company, New York, 1929). Copyright 1929, 1957 by The Macmillan Company.

[7] *Ibid.*, pp. 141–142.

A Bibliographical Note

T his bibliographical appendix is not a summary or even a
survey of the literature on the businessman's social responsibilities. It is intended for the receptive but still sus-
picious reader: the person who finds himself partially persuaded but not yet convinced by the arguments of this book.
He will find here material for further reading and reflection.

Reinhold Niebuhr's *Moral Man and Immoral Society*
(Charles Scribner's Sons, New York, 1932), though written
more than thirty-five years ago, is still the definitive critique of
those who rely upon "goodwill" to harness social power to the
requirements of justice. We acknowledge our fundamental
debt to Niebuhr and to this book in particular, despite the
fact that Niebuhr himself would probably dissent sharply from
our conclusion that the market effectively controls economic power. Niebuhr has argued this issue with Kenneth

Boulding, a distinguished economic theorist, in the latter's excellent contribution to the Council of Churches' series on ethics and economic life, *The Organizational Revolution* (Harper & Row, Publishers, Incorporated, New York, 1953).

Ethicists and moral theologians have been notoriously hostile to the idea that economic competition can promote social justice. This prejudice, if we may call it that, has been ably analyzed by the French economist Daniel Villey. His profound yet lucid article on "The Market Economy and Roman Catholic Thought," in *International Economic Papers*, no. 9, translated from the French by Jacques Kahane (The Macmillan Company, New York, 1959), deserves to be known by Protestant as well as Roman Catholic social theorists. Unfortunately, the relatively obscure place of its English publication has caused it to be generally overlooked.

The issue here is much more a matter for economic than for ethical analysis, involving as it does a correct interpretation and assessment of such phenomena as markets, competition, and maximizing activity. Were it not for the fact that Milton Friedman's reputation for "extremism" has made him *persona non grata* to those most in need, his *Capitalism and Freedom* (The University of Chicago Press, Chicago, 1962) could be recommended as an excellent antidote to some of the more persistent and pernicious misconceptions. A short article covering the essential ground is Jack Hirshleifer, "Capitalist Ethics: Tough or Soft?" *Journal of Law and Economics* (October, 1959). If we were more modest, we would not append to this list our own little book, *The Christian Encounters the World of Economics* (Concordia Publishing House, St. Louis, 1965). It should not be but probably is necessary to add that one can abandon antimarket prejudices without accepting *laissez faire* or concluding that the market system has no defects.

The economic limitations of the social responsibility doctrine have been set forth with wit and wisdom by Ben W.

Lewis, "Economics by Admonition," *American Economic Review* (May, 1959). Among noneconomists, the most incisive critic has been Theodore Levitt, "The Dangers of Social Responsibility," *Harvard Business Review* (September–October, 1958), and "Are Advertising and Marketing Corrupting Society?" *Advertising Age* (Oct. 6, 1958). Howard Bowen's *Social Responsibilities of the Businessman* (Harper & Row Publishers, Incorporated, New York, 1953) largely defends the social responsibility doctrine. His book is mentioned here not in an effort to present both sides, but because it is probably the most careful and comprehensive statement of the other view. The reader can hardly fail to discover that Bowen, too, has his doubts.

A crucial question (see Chapter VI) is that of the extent of monopoly or oligopoly in the United States today. There is a vast literature on this question. A representative and readable sample may be found in Edwin Mansfield (ed.), *Monopoly Power and Economic Performance* (W. W. Norton & Company, Inc., New York, 1964). The reader who wishes to pursue the question further can find ample leads in this book or in textbooks such as Clair Wilcox, *Public Policies toward Business*, 3d ed. (Richard D. Irwin, Inc., Homewood, Ill., 1966). For the reader in a hurry, the brief review article by Solomon Fabricant, "Is Monopoly Increasing?" *Journal of Economic History* (Winter, 1953), establishes the essential point: There is no longer any excuse for accepting the *assumption* of growing monopoly upon which so much of the social responsibility doctrine is built.

The reader who wonders what businessmen are thinking and saying about this issue will find some answers in Bowen's book, in Raymond C. Baumhart, "How Ethical Are Businessmen?" *Harvard Business Review* (July–August, 1961), and in John W. Clark, *Religion and the Moral Standards of American Businessmen* (South-Western Publishing Company, Cincinnati, 1966). The reader must remember, however, that what businessmen *say* is a clue, not a sure guide, to what they *think.* A pinch of salt if not of cynicism should be taken along with these studies.

A number of very excellent critical studies will be found in Earl F. Cheit (ed.), *The Business Establishment* (John Wiley & Sons, Inc., New York, 1964). Some of the articles, especially the contributions of John William Ward and Henry Nash Smith, offer particularly fresh perspectives as they begin to go beyond criticism toward constructive reinterpretation of the businessman's role in society.

And this is what the contemporary American businessman needs. It would not do for him to resist the social responsibility virus by succumbing to its antibody, a doctrine of irresponsibility. A healthy frame is the best defense against disease. The businessman needs a more adequate understanding of his world if he is to appreciate his proper role in it. More valuable to him than preachments on ethics and responsibility are such books as Edward S. Mason (ed.), *The Corporation in Modern Society* (Harvard University Press, Cambridge, Mass., 1961); Martin Mayer, *Wall Street: Men and Money* (Harper & Row, Publishers, Incorporated, New York, 1955), and *Madison Avenue, U.S.A.* (Harper & Row Publishers, Incorporated, New York, 1958); Leonard R. Sayles (ed.), *Individualism and Big Business* (McGraw-Hill Book Company, New York, 1963); or the perceptive reflections of John N. Brooks, *The Fate of the Edsel and Other Business Adventures* (Harper & Row, Publishers, Incorporated, New York, 1963). Another enormous intellectual debt would fail to receive adequate acknowledgment if we did not add three items from the pen of Alfred North Whitehead: his essays "Foresight," in *Adventures of Ideas* (The Macmillan Company, New York, 1933), "Technical Education and Its Relation to Science and Literature," and "Universities and Their Function," the latter two reprinted in *The Aims of Education and Other Essays* (The Macmillan Company, New York, 1929). The relevance of these essays to the businessman's understanding of his contemporary role and function will be appreciated by anyone fortunate enough to have discovered them.

Ethical discourse which is committed to the notion that ethics consists in adherence to rules will rarely escape from the realm of the trivial. This is a fatal flaw in most of the literature on ethics and the businessman. If the ethical discussion in this book succeeds at all in rising above moralistic platitudes, it is due to the influence of such men as Reinhold Niebuhr, Erich Fromm, David Riesman, Joseph Wood Krutch, Lewis Mumford, and, above all, the late Paul Tillich. The extent to which Tillich's thought, especially his *Love, Power and Justice* (Oxford University Press, Fair Lawn, N.J., 1954), has influenced this book will be obvious to anyone familiar with Tillich's work. For the rest we shall only mention Niebuhr, *The Nature and Destiny of Man* (Charles Scribner's Sons, New York, 1949); Fromm, *Man for Himself* (Holt, Rinehart and Winston, Inc., New York, 1947); Riesman, *Individualism Reconsidered* (The Free Press of Glencoe, New York, 1954); Krutch, *Human Nature and the Human Condition* (Random House, Inc., New York, 1959); and Mumford, *The Human Prospect*, edited by Harry T. Moore and Karl W. Deutsch (Secker and Warburg, London, 1956).

The reader is urged to examine these sources for himself and under no circumstances to condemn the prophets for the ineptitude or wrong headedness of a disciple.

Index